BAD VIBES

Luke Haines was born in God's own county of Surrey in 1967. He has recorded five albums with the Auteurs, one album as Baader Meinhof, three albums with Black Box Recorder, one film soundtrack album and two solo albums. He has appeared on *Top of the Pops* and has been nominated for loads of awards but has won nothing. In 2003 Luke Haines was in *Debretts People of Today*. He thinks that he is no longer listed in this esteemed publication, as the free copy of the magazine hasn't been delivered for some time. It's not the end of the world. The author is married with one child.

Luke Haines

BAD VIBES

Britpop and My Part in its Downfall

WILLIAM HEINEMANN: LONDON

Published by William Heinemann 2009

4 6 8 10 9 7 5 3

This book is substantially a work of non-fiction based on the life, experiences and recollections of the author. In some limited cases (notably Chapter 31) names of people/places/dates and the detail of events have been changed solely to protect the privacy of others.

First published in Great Britain in 2009 by
William Heinemann
Random House, 20 Vauxhall Bridge Road,
London SW1V 2SA

www.rbooks.co.uk

Addresses for companies within The Random House Group Limited can be found at:
www.randomhouse.co.uk/offices.htm

The Random House Group Limited Reg. No. 954009

A CIP catalogue record for this book
is available from the British Library

ISBN 9780434018468

The Random House Group Limited supports The Forest Stewardship Council (FSC), the leading international forest certification organisation. All our titles that are printed on Greenpeace approved FSC certified paper carry the FSC logo. Our paper procurement policy can be found at: www.rbooks.co.uk/environment

Typeset in Perpetua by Palimpsest Book Production Limited,
Grangemouth, Stirlingshire

Printed and bound in Great Britain by
CPI Mackays, Chatham, ME5 8TD

For Sian and Fred with love

Contents

Introduction

Back in August 2006, on the second night of my one-man show at the Edinburgh Festival, I was apprehended by a literary editor, several film producers, a crime writer and a prison officer and asked when my life story was coming out. I took the question as a fait accompli, as I do with most artistic endeavours that tickle my fancy, caught the train back to London and promptly did nothing about it. Six months later, while watching from the sidelines as my old record label (Virgin/EMI) crumbled, and recovering from the psychic wounds inflicted after a ghastly legal battle with yet another unscrupulous independent record label, I figured that now was the right time to write this memoir of my last decade in the twentieth century. Now that the house in the country, the sports car (with a boot not even big enough to hold my bespoke suits) and my last flush of youth had all gone, it was time to revisit the scene of a few old crimes. The book wrote itself.

The 90s: specifically 1992–7, which the body of this book is concerned with. The 90s: the dawn of post-fucking-everything, when I was in my twenties and my ego and I roamed about the globe, bickering and bitching like a couple of bad-tempered ogres. When I sat down to write this memoir I was surprised how much of this stuff was ricocheting about in my subconscious: youth, ambition, failure, depression, excess, spite and stupidity. Now I think it has stopped. I am a recovering egomaniac.

My twenties: when I was young and cruel. I want to stress that in writing this memoir I have spared the reader the dubious benefit of good old hindsight. The wisdom I have added is that dreadful, creeping brand of morning-after sobriety, which I hope gives a far more accurate insight into my mindset during this period. All of which should be enough to reassure the reader that *Bad Vibes* is emphatically *not* an exercise in score settling, though due to the 'in the moment transmission of my life' style in which this book is written the casual reader may beg to differ. It is very much what I thought then, not necessarily what I think now. We have to tell the truth. Do we not? Also, I should state that I bear no ill will to the people and characters in this book, most of whom I don't think about very often. When I do, it is only with fondness. Mostly.

Prologue

Is it ever right to strike a dwarf?

A strange thing happens at the beginning of 1993. I become a pop star. In France. Served up with the cornflakes. This turn of events takes everyone, not least of all me, by surprise.

My debut album – that is, the first album that I have written, played the lion's share of instruments on, arranged, and co-produced – *New Wave* is released in the UK and France simultaneously on 22 February 1993. In Blighty things are going swimmingly, better than I ever expected, but in France I am a palpable star. So much of a star that I idly toy with the idea of taking French lessons to improve my useless franglais. As it turns out, I'm just too busy pursuing my glamorous jet-setting lifestyle to do any thing as mundane as improve my continental linguistic prowess. I spend my honeymoon year of pop wonderment hurtling back and forth between London and France. *Perhaps the record company will rent me an apartment here in Paris? The 6th arrondissement would be nice.*

For the first few months after its release *New Wave* flies out of Fnac (record) stores the length and breadth of the republic at a rate of 10,000 copies a week. I am therefore required, by the laws of record promotion, to swim in the Gallic mainstream. Throughout the year I haughtily work my way through a glut of French television variety shows, appearing alongside jugglers, clowns, impressionists, ancient chansonniers, gifted pets, strippers and disturbed child stars. It's a fucking blast. I even get to do press conferences, where I get to try out my sarky Dylan – in *Don't Look Back* – act on the ladies and gentlemen of the foreign press. For them my success is not such a fucking blast. Things are going well.

So, in the halcyon summer of '93, I find myself in Strasbourg, midway through our second headlining tour of France. The venue is sold out. The continental heat only heightens the expectations of the crowd. We, the Auteurs, played a storming set here just a few months ago and now tonight's lucky ticket holders want more of the old magic. It won't be hard, I say to myself – the band's sound is supremely confident, and I'm surfing wave upon wave of the stuff. *Tonight, ladies and gentlemen, Strasbourg is mine.*

We're just hitting the penultimate song – the as yet unreleased 'Lenny Valentino' – when I notice the audience surging forward. A dwarf has been hoisted to the front of the crowd. Man, that midget is ugly – and badly dressed – I think to myself, taking in his mullet, designer stubble and brightly coloured European leisurewear. Drunk too. Within seconds the little man is kicking my shins and biting my knees. I am now sharing the stage with an unfashionable, drunken and extremely aggressive dwarf.

I look across at the other members of my band to gauge their facial expressions and to confirm that this is really happening. It is: Alice Readman, our bassist and my girlfriend, is mortified. The Cellist has his head bowed. I glance behind me at Barney C. Rockford, our drummer, to see that even though he is in hysterics, he is still ably pounding away at his kit. I wonder what facial expression I should adopt, but it's difficult to know how to react when one is being viciously attacked by a dwarf in front of many people.

The stage is high enough to give the audience a clear view of the unfolding farce, and 2000 French fans stare at me in horror. They came here to commune with their songwriting genius hero, not see him upstaged by a fucking midget. By now the ugly troll is bouncing around – a demented little rubber man. He's not drunk, he's utterly smashed. I start the guitar intro to 'Early Years' and kneel down to dwarf level, so that I at least look like I am complicit in this awful scenario. My gambit fails. It now looks as though I am serenading the diminutive cunt. The audience are enjoying this unedifying spectacle even less than I am, so I rise to my full height. The laughing gnome turns to face the audience and dances mockingly in front of me. I wonder how hard I can kick him without killing him. If my Chelsea-booted foot can connect with his small arse then I can probably hoof the fucker far out into the crowd like a rugby ball. I bring my leg back and am just about to exert full force when the cavalry arrives. General Custer in an Emerson Lake and Palmer world tour T-shirt strides across the stage: Big Neil, our tour manager. At six foot six, the tallest man in the building. Big Neil does what he has been dreading having to do. He gently picks the little fella up – legs furiously pedalling in the air as he is lifted high into the lighting gantry – carries him offstage and deposits him outside the venue. The Auteurs take a bow to muted applause. I never return to Strasbourg. *Served up with the cornflakes?* French toast more like.

1

You look like a star but you're still on the dole

1986–91. In 1986 the NME releases C86, *a state-of-the-nation cassette featuring among others Primal Scream, the Wedding Present and a west London group called the Servants. Elsewhere in 1986 the UK music press busy themselves by salivating over not-as-clever-as-they-think-they-are Sonic Youth and pretending to actually listen to the Butthole Surfers. By 1987 large swathes of the British public are contravening the natural impulse to be alone and are engaging in something called the 'second summer of love'. Steve Albini's new group are called Rapeman. By the end of the year Morrissey and Marr will split up the Smiths over an argument about Cilla Black. The real pop charts will be dominated by Stock, Aitken and Waterman, who between 1987 and 1990 have 12 number-one hit singles in the UK and have a penchant for likening themselves to Motown. August 1991 sees the first album release by Blur.*

Lawrence from Felt, Pete Astor from the Weather Prophets, Bobby Gillespie, Alan McGee, Grant McClennan and Robert Forster from the Go Betweens. In their own minds these men are rock royalty (the notion of indie does not yet exist). David Westlake and myself sit at the end of the table awaiting our turn. Nineteen years old. Winter 1987. Pre-gig pints in the Devonshire Arms, Camden Town. Shane MacGowan's manor – he's in the corner. This is pre-money London Town. When the place was still a shithole. The pubs all close at three in the afternoon for a few hours and there are only four channels on the TV. How did I get here?

Straight from school to art college, where after one year on a foundation course I am thrown out – *asked to leave* as I have 'a bad attitude to further education'. Not true. I have a great attitude. I blag a place at the London College of Music in Great Marlborough Street – a make-do for those not good enough to get into the Royal College of Music or Guildhall – leave my parents' home in Portsmouth and head for my first rented room, in Stockwell, south London.[1] Just in time for the first weekend of the 1985 Brixton riots. My housemates, Chad and Ange are manic dole fiends. We get drunk on looted lager from the Sunshine Supermarket on Railton Road. Then, with a little bit of Dutch, we head out and watch the final embers of Brixton burning (Ange Doolittle will have a small bite of fame as lead singer with late-80s band Eat).

I have not yet turned 18. Music college was everything I hoped it wouldn't be. Like every teenage Velvets nut with a guitar I hold on to the hope that I will meet a John Cale to play opposite my Lou Reed, naturally. Time, time. Running and passing. Got to get something together before I'm 19. November 1986. I answer an advert in *Melody Maker* for the first and only time: 'Servants singer songwriter seeks musicians'. The songwriter's name is David

[1] I was born in Walton-on-Thames in Surrey on 7 October 1967. My parents moved to Portsmouth when I was 14.

Westlake. I obsessively read the weekly music press (there are still four weekly music papers) so I have heard of his band the Servants. He has just sacked them. Westlake and I hit it off, and we're into the same stuff: the Modern Lovers, *Dragnet* and *Totales Turns* by the Fall. The Only Ones' first album. *Adventure* by Television. Wire and the Go Betweens. By March '87 I am in Greenhouse Studios, Islington playing guitar and piano on Westlake's first solo album, destined to be released on the then fashionable Creation label. By the end of the year the album *Westlake* is out and greeted with a yawn of indifference by a world far more interested in Ecstasy and the latest incarnation of the Manchester scene.[2] We, perhaps unwisely, revert to the old band name the Servants.

Lawrence from Felt, Bobby Gillespie, Alan McGee, Grant McClennan, Robert Forster, David Westlake and me. Men convinced of their own genius, though at 19 I am not yet a man, and it is strange to keep on meeting people who are almost ten years older. Pete Astor is the lead singer of the Weather Prophets, a Creation band who had their hour in the sun some six months ago. Pete's got the look and the regulation leathers. Ex-music journalist Pete has also got a theory on all rock 'n' roll lore. Just as well because the one thing he ain't got is the fucking songs. Bobby Gillespie wafts around saying little apart from who looks cool and who doesn't. Strangely people take notice of him. You're just too hip baby.

Tonight the Servants are supporting Lawrence's band Felt at Dingwalls. It is one of Felt's many farewell gigs to an indifferent nation. It will be a few years before Lawrence gets good and

[2] Mid-'88. David Westlake and I are laughing about the previous evening's debut TV performance by a hopeless new group called the Stone Roses. The show's presenter Anthony H. Wilson is very enthusiastic. The Servants; always a haven for sentient thought.

delivers his neo-glam masterpiece *Back in Denim*. Tonight, in the Devonshire, he is a classic study of fabulous rock star egotism in a hideous harlequin-motif jacket. Up his own enigma. Lawrence – a rock star in mind only – travels with a small entourage. A lackey is always on hand to light Lawrence's steady flow of cigarettes, as the Felt singer pontificates in a Brummie monotone – to no one in particular – on the possibilities of 'sewing on a fringe'. You see, Lawrence has started to lose his hair and does not have the money for an Elton-style transplant. The somewhat unlikely option of sewing on a fringe has become an obsession. In later years he will, on occasion, sport a hazardous wig. Photo sessions and video shoots will be at the mercy of the wig and its inability to cope with inclement weather. On and on he goes. Another cigarette is lit. The lackeys are giving Lawrence's fringe predicament some serious consideration.

Unfortunately any suggestions provoke petulant fits from the eccentric genius. I don't want to be complicit in high-maintenance Lawrence mania, so I move over to Grant's table. Grant McClennan of the Go Betweens has become a mentor to David and me, pushing 30 and proud of his elder statesmanship to the assembled Creation mob. Alan McGee loves the Go Betweens; he even names his forgettable mini-Malcolm McClaren scam girl band, Baby Amphetamine, after an Only Ones fanzine that Robert Forster and Grant put together back in their native Brisbane. Thankfully McGee's respect is not reciprocated. Tonight Grant is on form and drinking like giddy up. The Go Betweens fly back to Australia for good the next morning, after a few tough years in unyielding, unforgiving 80s London. Tonight is partly a farewell drink for them. 'It's great to be here tonight with all my favourite English bands who all wanna sound like the Byrds and the Velvet Underground,' muses Grant. 'Y'know, Creation is my third-favourite record label,' he adds with heavy sarcasm, rubbing McGee's face in it.

Alan McGee, anointer of genius and self-styled record mogul. I first met McGee back in the spring of '87, in Fury Murrays, a hellhole of a club behind Glasgow Central station. I am sound-checking my brand new Fender Telecaster. A Fender Telecaster I have scrimped and paid for in saved dole money and starvation. Hard won. If anyone so much as looks at this guitar in the wrong way they will unleash the winds of psychic war. Westlake and I are on the Scottish leg of a tour supporting the Weather Prophets. McGee sidles up to the front of the stage and points at me. 'You. You're Tom Verlaine.' He is of course referring to the buzz-saw blitzkrieg maverick lead guitarist of seminal symbolist New York City art rockers Television. Maybe some people would be happy with this introduction. Not I. I am a stickler for manners and would have preferred a 'How do you do?' or even a simple 'Hello.' The 80s were plagued by these small-time indie Svengalis, wannabe Brain Epsteins or mini-Malcolms. Forever proclaiming some poor bugger to be a genius. Of course hype is fundamental to pop music. But it often says more about the hyper than the hyped. The start of the cursed holy bestowals.

'You. You're Tom Verlaine,' it says, utterly unbecoming. I fix the fool with a dead-eyed stare. *Say nothing, say nothing*. You, Alan McGee, will pay for this transgression. You will pay.

Back in the Devonshire Arms Grant McClennan turns to me and whispers, loud enough for anyone to hear, 'That Alan McGee, not much going on up top.'[3]

Westlake, McClennan and I stagger up the road the 200 yards

[3] If McGee had really known his onions he would have realised that Tom Verlaine played a Fender Jaguar. It was Richard Lloyd who played the Telecaster.

or so to the venue. The old long bar of Dingwalls. Robert Forster is in the shadows. Thirty years old and a lean six foot four. Always conspicuous. Forster has just come out of his Prince phase. His new look is somewhere between *Raw Power*-period Iggy and Sherlock Holmes. With his long hair dyed silver grey – a homage to *Dynasty*'s Blake Carrington no less – round wire-frame glasses and tweed cape. This is a bold, potentially tragic look, but Forster carries it off. People just gaze in admiration. David Westlake and I are in awe of the man. Everybody loves Robert Forster, and no one can quite work out why he is not a huge star. He has hit a creative peak, having just written some of the best songs of his career – 'The Clarke Sisters', 'When People Are Dead', 'The House That Jack Keroauc Built'. A few hours earlier, back in the Devonshire, Pete Astor delivered a lecture on why all Robert's new songs are merely 'filler material'. Yeah, yeah, Pete. Whatever you say.

We do the gig. Too drunk to play well, we still – in the rock 'n' roll vernacular – blow Felt off the stage. Everyone talks loudly through Felt's set. Lawrence is playing his latest epic, 'Primitive Painters'. On and on it goes. Somewhere, fresh paint dries upon a wall. Sadly, I am not there to watch it.

More drinks at the bar with Robert, Grant and Lindy Morrison, the Go Betweens' terrifyingly blunt drummer. 'If you're gonna play Dingwalls you've gotta fucken rock. Lemmy hangs out here with fucken Johnny Thunders. You can't play like a bunch of fucken pussies. You've gotta fucken rock.' She has a point.

Lawrence. Pete Astor. Bobby Gillespie. Alan McGee. Grant McClennan. Robert Forster. David Westlake. Me. All of these men convinced of their own genius. One of these men now sadly dead.[4]

*

[4] On Saturday 6 May 2006 Grant McClennan died in his sleep at his Brisbane home. He is sorely missed.

Four long years later. October 1991. Four years of recording songs that no one hears. Gigs that no one attends. Photographs that no one sees. Four long years of income support. Restart interview, income support, restart interview, income support, restart interview. Enterprise Allowance scheme, Mrs Thatcher's ingenious new 'arts grant' – David Westlake and I get one each. Four long years and one single, in '89 called 'It's My Turn' (it isn't), and one album – existential art rock, ten years too late and fifteen years too early – called, with unflinching self-knowledge – *Disinterest* (1990). Four long years. Six bass players, three drummers and two uninterested record labels. We have perfected haircuts that no one will look at. We practise quotes for interviews that will never take place. This is of course what all healthy rock 'n' roll 20-year-olds must do. Trouble is I am now 24. David is 26. We have reached the end of our rope. We painstakingly record demos for one more album, provisionally entitled – and again with self-awareness not lacking – *Smalltime*. The demos are great, but the album never gets made. What little luck there was ran out long ago, and in October '91 the Servants call it a day.

Four long years. Bad habits die hard. In my sloth I've picked up a few. On a dreary Tuesday autumn afternoon I line up three bottles of red wine. Three bullets, each with my name on. Russian roulette with all the chambers loaded. I down the bottles in just over two hours. I could probably do more but I'm wearier than usual. I pass out on the couch. I dream about red. Swathes of crimson red. I am Isadora Duncan, in a red car, on a red road, with a red sky, and a red scarf caught in a red wheel tightening around my neck. My skinny long dancer's neck. I'm thrown out of a feverish sleep by the need to vomit. Blood. Throwing up fucking blood. I am by nature a hypochondriac, but to have an irrational fear of death turn into the actual possibility of dying is quite something. Without too much prompting I see a scornful doctor. A severe eastern European lady of retirement age prods at my sides and back. Tuts and shakes her head. Dispassionately she tells me what I already know. That I most probably have serious liver damage. (Tests confirm this.) All self-inflicted. Give up drinking and smoking. Or die.

2

First blood

November 1991–May 1992. The Auteurs' first demos recorded November/ December 1991 as Nirvana's second album Nevermind *heads to the top of the charts on both sides of the Atlantic. American rock rules: Soundgarden from Seattle, Smashing Pumpkins and Pavement are loved by all. In March 1992* Melody Maker *puts Suede on the front cover before they have a record out, calling them 'The Best New Band In Britain'. Their debut single 'The Drowners', released in May, hits number 49 in the UK singles chart.*

It is strange to come face to face with your own mortality when barely into your mid-twenties. I spend sober days staring out of the kitchen window watching the overgrown garden creep up on me. John Cale's 1982 semi-improvised howl of drunken pain, *Music for a New Society*, clatters away in the background. It doesn't help. Perhaps if I stay here long enough in my vegetative state the garden will engulf me and bury me alive. I share a large ground-floor flat in far-flung suburban Southgate, north London with Alice. I am convinced this is the flat I shall expire in. Luckily for Alice, she is doing a full-time degree course in film and art history at nearby Middlesex Poly, so she is spared the misery of my morbid unemployed existence. Some people when faced with their own mortality choose to spend what may be their last days leading a hedonistic debauched lifestyle; others embrace religion and an ascetic existence, atoning for their sins in preparation for the inevitable. Or maybe take care of practical matters. Perhaps arrange the funeral – after all, it won't arrange itself. I choose to write an album. God knows why. Rock 'n' roll hasn't got me anywhere before, unless you count my sorry predicament.

I am a cell of one. Great art must be created in isolation. Hermetically sealed. Art. Black art. Art speaks with fork tongue. Bullshit art. Explain yourself. Are you a savant? Perhaps a cipher? Channelling the voices of dead souls – just like Ian Curtis. A noble savage. Art speaks with fork tongue. I am a cell of one.

Creating art is like building a wall. Don't let anyone tell you otherwise. Writing a great song is like building a wall, or whittling at best. I work in ascetic denial. All I allow myself to listen to is a cassette: *Golden Hour with the Kinks. The Original Modern Lovers* is already etched on my brain. Songs come slowly but they do at least come. 'Bailed Out' and 'Don't Trust the Stars' (a poke at the millennial obsession with astrology and mumbo-jumbo) are early front runners, then 'Starstruck'. A breakthrough. A feather-light ballad from the point of view of a washed-up child star.

When you finally crack it, the self-doubt drains away, so I seize my moment and write for all I'm worth. 'Early Years' is a fictional account of those hungry times in the Servants. 'Showgirl' a rags-to-rags glitter fantasy written on a train journey from Guildford to Waterloo. Another faded glamour vignette about a loser marrying an off-off-Broadway actress. There is not a shred of truth in it. Yet it's still a classic.

I quickly learn how to use a four-track tape recorder. With limited resources – a couple of guitars, an out-of-tune upright piano, cardboard boxes for drums, a Pixiephone, finger cymbals and a delay pedal – I make myself work nine to five each day, while Alice is at college. I find that by recording the piano backwards I can make it sound like a cello. By December I have a demo tape. A demo tape that's murky and wobbly but undeniably magical. Christ, even I'd buy this. I start daydreaming about my primordial stew of stately English ballads, which sounds like a wake for Tyrannosaurus Rex[5] and the Incredible String Band. The songs are well on their way to greatness, even the cardboard boxes thudding away in the soup sound cool. These early recordings are like nothing else currently around.

In a Christmas boozer I stumble into an old school pal. Glenn Collins is that rare thing, a young person who is genuinely eccentric. He buzzes around the pub in a horrible tweed suit and spats, puffing away on a briar pipe. It's a maverick look for sure. Glenn spends his life tinkering with vintage British motorbikes. Motorbikes that will forever remain stationary in his drive. He dreams of being an antique dealer. Almost predictably, he claims to have been caught up in some sort of alien abduction and earns a paltry living as a gardener. A *gardener*. Glenn Collins is as mad as a budgerigar. He is also a drummer, a drummer who has the Howard Kaylan/Mark Volman backing vocals thing off pat. Glenn is a rare breed. For this I like him a lot. A few days later I play him my little demo tape. First track 'Starstruck'. He thinks it's a hit single. He's in. Like I said, mad as a budgie.

*

[5] In particular, Tyrannosaurus Rex's underrated *Beard of Stars* from 1970. Practically a Marc Bolan solo album.

Early 1992. I'm sitting in a burnt-out flat in Dalston, east London. Dave Barker is the owner of the flat. Thirty-eight years old and a dead ringer for Brian Wilson during the bedbound years. Barker has been given his own imprint on Fire Records. The Servants made a record for Glass, Dave's old label back in '88. Dave Barker is fundamentally a good guy who loves the records he puts out. He just has great difficulty getting anything done. His fire-damaged flat reeks of smoke. A few months ago Dave fell asleep in his armchair. Fag in hand, turning the one-bedroom purpose-built into an inferno. Dave Barker is a man who is lucky to be alive. His pet cat wasn't so lucky. Incinerated.

'She 'ad bronchitis anyway,' he adds pragmatically.

'I'm not surprised, Dave,' I say, nodding at the overflowing ashtray. Dave's throat and lips combine with a throaty gurgle to make a noise that passes for laughter.

I haven't seen Dave for about a year; now his life seems to have turned into a Tom Waits song.

My mission is twofold. I need to get a gig for my as yet unnamed band. I am also aware that I am still under contract with Fire Records.

When Glass inevitably ran out of money, Barker remortgaged his house in a bid to keep the label going. Dave's indolence meant that injection of money didn't last long, and soon Glass Records tanked. Clive Solomon, who owns Fire, is a notorious figure in the music industry. Clive buys Dave's old label and also offers Dave a job at Fire. Unfortunately when Barker goes to Fire he also takes the Servants with him. When bands get desperate they do dumb things. In 1990 the Servants signed to Fire Records. Forever.

The master plan is to get Dave Barker to release me from the contract. He will feel bad about this and offer me a gig by way of compensation. I am sure Dave will hate my demo. It's the polar opposite of all the third-rate feedback-churning cack that he is so in love with. I walk over to Dave's stereo and put the unnamed tape on. Just to seal the deal I tell Barker that my new band is called Youth Movement. It's a piss-poor name, the worst that I can think of. 'Fuckin' 'ell, that's a fuckin' terrible name,' chokes Dave. Ace in the hole. 'Fuckin' great songs though. Didn't know you 'ad it in you.'

Thanks, Dave. Dave Barker. From Romford, Essex. I leave the flat with a gig, opening for the Television Personalities. I am still under contract. I know that Dave will be too lazy to play the songs to Clive Solomon. I expect I'll be stuck in contractual limbo with Fire Records forever. For now I put it out of my mind. There is, at least, a gig to prepare for. These little matters, such as being signed to an overtly hostile record label, do tend to come back to haunt you.

As a precocious teen I had worked my way through the classics of European cinema. Goddard's *Weekend* – yeah, yeah. *The Discreet Charm of the Bourgeoisie* – sure. *Jules et Jim* – tick. It's amazing how you get ideas above your station when you live in the provinces. Alice is reading up on new wave French cinema as part of her degree. *Cahiers du Cinéma*. Auteur theory. Fuck, how did I miss this stuff? Actually it's deathly dull, but the name jumps out from the page. The Auteurs. It is one of the all-time great band names. Like the Supremes or the Monkees, but for intellectual snobs. It's even a contradiction in terms. Perfect. So the Auteurs it is. I persuade Alice to pick up the bass guitar again – during the last dark days of the Servants she was press-ganged into bass duties and now has a pretty good grasp of the instrument – and Glenn transports our equipment around in a gardening trailer. We rehearse hell for leather.

Early 90s London is full of derivative charmless bands clogging up the live circuit. Everybody seems to be in thrall to the American bands on the ultra hip Sub Pop label, TAD and Mudhoney. Dinosaur Junior are lauded on a weekly basis. Nirvana's instant classic *Nevermind* is everywhere. I am working on a new song called 'American Guitars': part sarcastic riposte to British bands who cannot find their own voice, forever worshipping at the altar of US rock, part self-mythologising history of my fledgling band. Soon the British press will pick up on 'American Guitars', proclaiming it some sort of battle cry against the marauding Yanks. It won't be long before Britpop rears its ugly head, bobbing about on the perimeters, then brazenly cavorting around on centre stage like an attention-seeking moron.

The Auteurs play their first gig at the Rock Garden in April. Later that month we support the Television Personalities at the Bull and Gate, Kentish Town. Our third gig is at the Euston Rails club in May.

The Euston Rails is a bar/canteen for London Underground employees situated on the forecourt of Euston station. It's great, and I'm in a fine mood for this gig. Throughout the soundcheck the monitor engineer gleefully insults my guitar sound. A good omen. Tonight the Auteurs are shockingly good. The previous two gigs had been tentative, but now we find our sound. After the show a young man approaches me. He babbles some nonsense and then gives me his card:

David Laurie
(wants to be an)
A & R man

One day he will be, but now what a cheeky scamp. Between nervous chortling Laurie tells me I should send a demo to Malcolm Dunbar at East West records, part of Warner Brothers. 'Don't send him one tape; send him ten or fifteen. Make sure he knows who you are.' Chancer. I raise Laurie and send 30 copies of my demo tape to Malcolm Dunbar. I also send a couple of copies to *NME* journalists Steve Lamacq and John Mulvey.

I'm optimistic after my offensive on East West, and I am feeling less deathly after months of temperance. A late-spring sunny afternoon and I come in from the garden of our Southgate flat to answer the telephone.

'Can I speak to Luke Haines please?'

'Speaking.'

'I'm calling on behalf of East West records. Would you give me your address so I can return your tapes?'

So the plague of tapes return to their creator. We only have one more gig lined up – at the Tufnell Park Dome in June. The East West rejection makes me realise that this is my last chance.

I have played the Tufnell Park Dome before, at some crappy Creation night back in the 80s. Tonight we are supporting a grizzled old biker band. For our turn there are about seven people in the audience. It doesn't matter: one of them is Steve Lamacq reviewing for the *NME*.

Thursday. Two days after the Dome gig. The phone rings.

'Hello, my name is Jon Eydmann. Can I speak to someone about the Auteurs?'

Oh Christ, another one wanting a return address.

'Malcolm Dunbar played me your demo. I manage a band called Suede. We'd really like you to support us on some dates in July . . . Oh, and Steve Lamacq has given you a rave review in the *NME*.'

Fucking A. I call up Glenn.

'We're supporting Suede in July.'

'Fuck. I love Slade.'

'No, you cunt. Suede.'

3

How to create a masterpiece

June–October 1992. Jimmy Nail's 'Ain't No Doubt' is number one for two weeks in July, followed by 'Rhythm Is a Dancer' by Snap. Also in July 1992 Laurence's new group Denim finish recording a debut album. It's good, and it's called Back in Denim. *In August the Auteurs begin recording their debut album,* New Wave. *The Shamen beguile us with 'Ebeneezer Goode', and Suede cop their first top-twenty hit in September with 'Metal Mickey'. The first Mercury Music Prize is won by Primal Scream for* Screamadelica.

It's gonna be a fine summer. I'm the new girl in town and everyone wants to fuck me. In his *NME* live review Steve Lamacq writes how great it would be if the Auteurs had a record out next week. About how my voice sounds like Steve Harley's (this is possibly the first time in the last ten years that anyone has used a reference to Harley in a positive way). It's a cool review for sure, and you know what? The phone doesn't stop ringing. Malcolm Dunbar calls. Jazz Summers, head of Big Life, calls. Saul Galpern from Nude (Suede's label) calls. Sony. Warners. Some guy from Atlantic

Records in New York keeps calling in the middle of the night. It's a fucking gas. As the week goes on, the phone is ringing off the hook. And then the grim reaper. I had been half expecting a call from the reaper since my visit to the quack. Pick up the phone. Receiver pressed against my ear.

'Hello, Luke,' says a most diabolical voice. 'It's Clive here. Clive Solomon.'

Clive Solomon is trying really hard to be the genial, reasonable, down-with-the-artists record company guy that we both know he is not. I have been invited over to his Stoke Newington townhouse to discuss my happy future with Fire Records. He is trying so damned hard to be nice that he looks like he's in physical pain. We are being very careful not to allude to the fact that we both know I am already signed to his label. Clive twitters on about how much he loves music (beware the ones who really live for their music) and how he wants me to record an album for Fire. Suspiciously he says he will give me an advance of £10,000. Why pay me an advance if I'm already signed? I wonder.

'Why not do some studio recordings right now? Oh, and by the way, can you do an interview with *Melody Maker* next week?' Clive, it would seem, is taking things for granted and getting ahead of himself. What can you do?

The bald man in front of me in short trousers, a music journalist, has decided that my band, the Auteurs, are the future of rock 'n' roll. He is trying to set us up as some kind of rivals to the already lauded Suede. On a sunny summer morning I am being interviewed by Steve Sutherland, editor of *Melody Maker*, in a dingy pub in Soho. Me, the brains behind the operation, Ian Brady to Suede's more compliant Hindley. I'm sharp as you like – off the sauce.

I've got loads of great quotes. Why wouldn't I have? I've been working on them for years. When the feature comes out, it reads like a testimonial. A testimonial for the Auteurs and Suede as an early Britpop alliance. I'm not too keen on being lumped in with Suede, there's too much of the *TSB Rock School* about them. But nevertheless back home the phone is ringing more than ever, and no one is asking for a return address.

Clive has fixed me up with a producer: Phil Vinall. Clive seems to think that Phil is the in-house producer for Fire Records. Phil Vinall (real name) is eight years older than me. He has worked in studios forever. Good chops. A young engineer in the early days of Stiff Records, he's a veteran of the Ruts and Public Image's *Metal Box* sessions. He's got the ulcer to prove it, and lives off milkshakes. In the last couple of years Phil has branched out as an independent producer. We click immediately. In the middle of June 1992 Alice, Glenn and I go into Falconer Studios in Kentish Town, with Vinall at the controls, and record three tracks in as many days. 'Starstruck', 'Bailed Out' and 'Early Years'. I am getting closer to the sound I want. I really should sort out the situation with Fire Records.

Things are moving fast. Fucking ring a ding ding. I am now so important that I screen all my calls – click on to answerphone message.

'Do you need a manager?' asks a voice on the tape.

Er. I think I probably need one of those. I wait a few hours and call the guy back. His name is Tony Beard. He's got a management company. Tony and his business partner have been attempting to resurrect the career of Peter Perrett. This alone is enough for me. Perrett cut two killer albums (and a half-arsed third one) with the Only Ones in the late 70s before marinating himself in smack. I give Tony the job. The job of extricating myself from the contract with Clive Solomon and Fire Records.

We arrive in Windsor late for our soundcheck. Glenn's wheezing old Datsun can only touch 50 on the motorway towing that fucking gardening trailer. Our crap equipment is jiggling about and the odd muddy twig finds its way into the back of an amplifier. As we pull up outside the venue Matt Osman, Suede's bass player, greets us. He is wearing a paper party hat. Cute little teddy bears dance around his head. The teddy bears of pop success. Things are clearly going well in his world. Matt is a smart cookie, and he puts his head in his hands when I casually mention the Clive Solomon situation.

'Get the fuck out of there. They'll fuck you up.' Thanks. Tell me something I don't know. Matt's rare wit gives him surprising clarity on the increasingly feverish adoration that is being heaped upon his band. The jovial bass player is also aware of the disparity between my group and his, and our pathetic mode of transport is the thing that is currently tickling his funny bone. He wanders along the side of the old Datsun with its trailer accessory, laughing merrily and pointing out all too obvious deficiencies. I do not join in. It's easy to laugh in a party hat as your roadies unload your expensive new equipment from your tour bus.

The Suedey boys saunter about their dressing room. They don't bother with false modesty; they're fucking full of it. I like that. They laugh at Glenn's spats – we all do – and in mocking silly voices sing my songs back to me. Half admiration, half piss-take. I don't care. I've heard their single and I know I can outwrite them. Brett's got a few good lines and knows there's a bit of mileage to be had in writing lyrics about 'retards' and 'dads', but overall they're just a little too reliant on the old wasted-glamour-in-council-estates routine. Writing about what you know isn't always the ticket. Live, they are a different prospect. We are playing toilets in the provinces and the little girls are coming out in force.

The press have a hard-on. For once they have actually championed a group that looks like it might sell records. Suede kick like a naughty mule, and Brett whips his arse with the microphone. He still looks like Jack Wilde's Artful Dodger from *Oliver*, but when he squeals his way through the numbskull classic 'Metal Mickey' the kiddies wet themselves and that old blues maxim 'The men don't know what the little girls understand' is proved yet again. We do our extremely cool thing. I play my new stalker song, 'Home Again'. It's a heavy breather call about breaking into a girl's house, looking through her belongings, reading her diary and opening an envelope containing test results. For added intensity, and in an attempt to unnerve the audience (and myself) I have taken to doing the song a capella.

Suede have got a couple of freaky fans: Eric and Karen. They follow Suede and us everywhere, two lunatics in the corner of every dressing room bickering. Apparently Karen is a little over-familiar for Eric's liking when addressing the band.

'They're not mere mortals like us, they're . . .' Eric is searching for a word. He doesn't want to have to say it out loud, but Karen's recent behaviour is forcing him to tell it like it really is. 'They're gods,' he finally blurts out. These two fruitcakes lead the vanguard of the Suedey poppets. What they say goes. So when the Auteurs play, the kids listen politely but do not go crazy. They tolerate us, they have to. We are the chosen guests of their new gods. Another bloody holy bestowal. Doesn't matter. *We hate you, little girls.*

July 1992. I'm pacing the Southgate flat in impotent rage. I've ripped the stuffing out of the fucked sofa, kicked a rotting door until it is mortally wounded and now I'm gonna duff up the kitchen. Ripping out the rickety drawers and hurling the contents around the room in fury. Alice will be staying out for a while. She knows there is no point trying to calm me down when I get like this. I've been drinking – for the first time in six months – since the letter arrived in the second post. The letter is a threat from Clive Solomon that if I try and sign with a label that is not Fire Records he will be forced to issue an injunction against me. Solomon signs off by going on about what good friends we have become, and how he can't believe the situation has got to this, blah blah. It's a weaselly trick at the end of a measly letter. Designed to get my goat. Goat got, I stumble off to buy more whisky, cursing at the unfairness of it all. The music industry is, for the first time, knocking at *my* door. En masse. Unfortunately one of those people knocking is Clive Solomon, who, if he gets his way, will effectively bury any chance I have. This whole spat with Clive has become a major fucking drag. For the past few weeks I've had to endure Solomon's lackeys bleating away on my answerphone, 'Is everything OK? Why won't you return our calls? You need to come in to the office and talk to us . . .'

Manager Tony is dealing with this impending shitstorm, but too slowly for my liking. The phone haranguing was one thing, but the letter has pushed all the buttons. My mood is nothing short of murderous. I must find my old Fire contract and *hope*, just hope, that I can find a way out of it. Hope, though, is the thing that will kill you. Right now I want to fucking kill Clive Solomon. So I sit on the floor of my trashed living room and drink until I pass out.

In one hand I have a torch and in the other a Stanley knife. I'm feeling good, like Stanley Baker in a caper movie. A highly moral English robber. I'm standing in the basement of Clive Solomon's townhouse, which he has turned into an aquarium. An aquarium filled with thousands of tiny angelfish. Nobody saw me break in, only a hissing tomcat. When I told the cat what I was doing he didn't seem that bothered. He just shrugged his shoulders and said, 'Do what you've got to do. Solomon's a right cunt.' I have come here to find my contract and to kill Clive Solomon. I shall enjoy killing him, for revenge and for fun. Cut the fucker up like Sharon Tate. Helter fucking skelter. A thousand dune buggies descending on Stoke Newington, murder madness Charlie Manson style. A light goes on upstairs – that bastard tomcat must have squealed on me, the fucker. There are so many fish tanks I can't decide which one to hide behind. I can hear footsteps getting closer. I stand stock still amid the fish, facing the huge velvet theatre curtains. I try and control my breathing, gripping hard on the Stanley knife and running my finger along the blade so that I draw blood. The curtains fly back and there in a golden dressing gown stands Clive Solomon, looking like the ghost of every awful Christmas rolled into one.

'What the fuck do you think you are doing?' screams Solomon. 'Did you really think you would get away with it,' continues the furious Svengali, before adding sinisterly, 'My cat is a quisling – he tells all – and you'll do time for this, lots of it, and when you're finally released, you'll still be mine.' Before I can respond, a diabolical primeval roar issues forth from above. A youngish man dressed in only a loincloth leaps from the rafters and lands in a squatting position before Solomon. It's an astonishing athletic feat. What's more, I recognise the young man smeared in warpaint. He's the lead singer of Pulp, Jarvis Cocker. Pulp have been on Solomon's label for years.

'Hold my glasses,' says Jarvis, as he thrusts his bins towards me. 'I am now about to give you a given signal,' continues the Pulp main man as if there are more people in the room. Jarvis gives a blood-curdling scream – my God it's terrifying – and, on cue, pale skinny young men appear from behind the fish tanks. Oh Christ, I've walked into an indie uprising, I think to myself as I survey this army of embittered rockers, more used to wielding Gretsch guitars than the arsenal of homemade weaponry they are now in charge of.

'I am now about to give another given signal,' says warrior Jarvis in what will become his characteristically dry style, before issuing the signal, another blood-curdling scream. 'Now kill the cunt!' roars the Pulp man, as he expertly hurls a home-made spear into the petrified Solomon's throat. They must have history, I muse as half a dozen indie rockers leap upon the record company mogul, smashing him over the bonce with broken bottles. Within seconds the fucker is dead. I walk over to the lifeless body and give it a soft kick in the side. An ancient parchment contract falls out of the corpse's dressing-gown pocket. Man, this night is really turning out swell. Not only have I got my contract, but the wicked witch is also a goner. I turn to say something to Jarvis, but he's busy.

'We must bleed him dry,' says man-of-the-people Jarvis to his followers. 'Come, let's commune' say's Pulp's frontman as he greedily guzzles a wine-glass full of Solomon's blood. Some people really do hate you, I think, as I climb over Clive Solomon's remains, which are now smoking and slowly dissolving. I let myself out the front door and see the treacherous cat looking sorry for himself. 'Let's forgive and forget,' I say. 'You were only doing your job.' The psychically dismantled tomcat has a tear in his eye. 'Come on, catty, lunch is on me.' I pick up the remorseful beast and sit him on my shoulder. Off we wander, home through a forest, to have lunch.

The much-sought-after contract miraculously turns up in a lawyer's office in late July, and Manager Tony unearths the small matter of a paltry amount of money due to the Servants upon signing with Fire Records: £250. The money was never paid. The stupid fucker, if he'd just given me that £250 I would have been his for life. I am free to walk away from Fire. (Others would not be so lucky.) For the moment I'm riding my luck.

I'm rather taken aback when I first meet David Boyd. Hut Recordings – a subsidiary of Virgin which is in turn owned by EMI – picks up the Auteurs' scent late in the chase in August

1992.[6] Manager Tony takes me in for a meeting with David and Ken Marshall, DB's sidekick from his old Rough Trade days. Ken has played Boyd the Auteurs' demo and now he's hot to trot. Oh man, this duo are unpromising: Dave sits on the floor, blonde hair longer and lanker than Rick Wakeman's and dressed in dungarees. An endless supply of joints gets passed around – at this stage I always decline – and Brother Ken goes googly eyed over the greatness of my demos. This could be any time between 1969 and 1976. We are adrift in a sea of denim. It's like having a meeting with the Doobie Brothers. Hut Recordings is situated in a tiny attic of Richard Branson's grand folly Vernon Yard – which ain't a yard, it's a mansion by the canal in Kensal Rise, west London. Up flight after flight of winding stairs, until you get to a door. On that door there is a sticker bearing the legend 'Corporate Rock Sucks'. Hut Recordings: it's a hippy shack.

In 1992 there is a certain uptightness about labels like Hut. 'They're fake independent labels. They're not in it for the music. We allow our bands to develop,' squeals the holier-than-thou indie Taleban. 'EMI have links with the arms trade. We operate a profit share you know,' drones the milksop Greek chorus. *Oh yeah. Well maybe I want to have links with the arms trade. Perhaps I don't want to share my profits with other bands on the label. Kind of you to presume that*

[6] Around mid-1992 Richard Branson sells the record label part of his empire – Virgin Records, famous for *Tubular Bells*, the Sex Pistols, etc. – to EMI. EMI retain the 'identity' and brand name Virgin. Also around this time Virgin/EMI starts up boutique labels from within the Virgin building to serve different markets. One of these labels is Hut Recordings. In 1992 major record labels are still unsure how to market groups that would otherwise be signed to independent labels. Hut Recordings, which looks and acts like an independent label but with EMI distribution and major label recording and marketing budgets, is an attempt to surmount this.

I'm some mealy mouthed peacenik socialist. I've just had five years of entanglement with pious indie labels, and the bottom line is that if you sign with *any* record label, whoever their paymasters may be, you are going to get ripped off, kiddo – maybe to a small extent, or maybe you'll lose your wife, dog and children. Major record labels just tend to be a bit more honest about ripping you off. It looks like I'm going to sign with Hut.

Hoxton Square. East London. A basement recording studio. Shoreditch is a wasteland – empty streets with no shops. Only shoe emporiums that remain closed. One pub, the Bricklayers Arms. No deejays, just a couple of old soaks who must have drifted in from nearby Whitechapel or perhaps Bethnal Green. The young people with their silly hats have not yet moved here. The artists lurk but fortunately have not yet made their presence felt. No man's land. Flanders. Alice and Glenn have recorded their parts. Now it's just Vinall and me. I know this is my moment. If I let it slip through my fingers now, I'll never have it again. The Hut deal is safe but taking time to sort out, so Manager Tony is bankrolling the album himself at a cost of ten grand. It's simple: Phil lets me do exactly as I like. He's Nick Lowe and I'm Elvis C. We record glockenspiels, finger cymbals, cardboard boxes (again) layer upon layer of acoustic guitar and walls of hand claps. Double-track everything. I'm still not used to the sound of my voice, so we triple-track it, smooth it out. Manicured and buffed. On days off we fit in extra support slots with Suede. At scenesters' pub the White Horse in Hampstead the new Fab Four announce that they will be playing on the roof. At a gig in the 100 Club a fan stands directly in front of me during our set. The fan is very keen to show me he knows all the lyrics to the yet-to-be released 'Early Years' by mouthing along with me. Backstage the fan introduces himself to me as 'a very powerful journalist from the *NME*'. Hahahaha. 'Me and my colleagues are going to do everything we can to help you,' crows the very powerful journalist from the *NME*. He is trying to be friendly but he shouldn't have bothered. I've seen this fool before, on some TV rock show, swanning around the *NME* office with a big hard-on about himself. These ugly-guy music journalists always conform to type. Speech impediment? Check. Bullied at school? Check. Amazing how the victim becomes the bully.

Back at the studio Phil has roped in Kuljit Bhamra, an Indian percussionist, who on occasion plays for the Aga Khan. Kuljit adorns 'Bailed Out' with tablas. It's killer in a very non-mystic, non-trippy way. I try my usual trick of recording the piano backwards to simulate a cello, but Phil's not buying it. Why not just get a cello player in; the budget can just about stand it.

So Phil brings the Cellist into the fold. We spend an afternoon adding cello to first 'Showgirl' and 'Bailed Out'. It sounds so on it that I add it to three more songs. 'Starstruck', 'How Could I Be Wrong', and 'Home Again'. That's it. Fully formed. We have our sound and I have, for better and worse, the Cellist. By the end of 1994 every other new band will also be adorning their records with cello.

I am sitting in our dressing room, high above the 2000 hysterical kids in some godforsaken town hall of a venue in Bradford. The Auteurs have just finished a short set in front of Suede's more demented northern fans. After merciless and ceaseless stage invasions I have taken a microphone stand in the mouth and am now minus one front tooth. I apply more pressure to my upper gum in a futile attempt to stop the torrent of blood that is unstoppable due to the tooth that once resided there now residing somewhere on the stage below. Matt Osman and Bernard Butler have joined us in the dressing room and show some concern for my welfare, or maybe they're just a little anxious. In quarter of an hour they too will have to face the braying mob downstairs, and they've seen the damage it is capable of.

'When we came in the venue tonight we looked at each other and said, "Is *that* noise the Auteurs? What the fuck has *happened* to them?"' says Matt. This is all meant in the most complimentary way. You see, we now rock hard. Way harder than before, and the kids in Bradford have lost their minds to our thoughtful noise. This is the first date of our one and only complete tour supporting Suede; the earlier tour only amounted to half a dozen dates before the headliners cancelled. If the crazed kids got the better of me, then Suede have no worries. As I watch the madness below from our dressing-room window, I realise why Suede are always so insistent that the Auteurs support them: because we will never be able to blow them offstage. This September/October tour is a riot. Suede are no longer the critics' favourite. They're now in the charts and at the vanguard of a teenage rampage. Most nights I bother to watch the headliners because they are now great: supercharged, violent and commanding. In years to come when the populace have been numbed into a stupor by the Britpop assizes, the genuine teen pop mayhem of the early Suede shows will be somewhat forgotten. But you know, right here, right now in September 1992, I'm genuinely grateful to be in the centre of this madness.

I've got a secret weapon: *New Wave*. My record's better than yours. I want to chant it in every new town that we roll into. To compound my joy I am also in possession of a leaked cassette of Suede's album. *Man, you lot have blown it big time*. It's the production: weedy, horrible phased guitars lost in a sea of cheapo reverb. The violent poovery of the live shows neutered by the recording studio. Of course, no one notices any of this when the record comes out (one month after the Auteurs' debut), and the record goes on to sell gazillions and be tagged with all those fastest-selling-debut-album-of-last-week-style statistics. We play our final support show with Suede in front of a packed house in some sort of colonial ballroom in Victoria. At the end of a happy celebratory evening – which feels like a homecoming of sorts – Bernard Butler and I promise to get together soon and write some songs. Of course we never do, but it's that kind of evening. Now it's time to extricate myself from the Suede orbit. The next time our paths cross will be at the Mercury Awards in a year's time.

Ten months ago I felt my number was up. Abstinence, I feel, has restored my fragile health, and activity has for the time being put an end to my hypochondria. I visit a different doctor – not the eastern European – and have more tests. Three weeks later I am given a clean bill of health. The tests show no sign of any liver damage, nor, the doctor adds cautiously, does it look like there was ever any sign of damage. The doctor implies that I am entitled to make an official complaint about the previous flagrant misdiagnosis. I don't bother. I don't wish to burden myself with reality or to open the door to mundanity. Besides I now wish to resume my career of chemical imbalance.

In late October 1992 the Auteurs sign a five-album deal with Hut Recordings. The album *New Wave* is complete, in every sense. It is everything I hoped it would be. Journalists phone up Manager Tony wanting to hear the album. Radio producers are clamouring for a sneak preview. They'll have to wait until the New Year. Alice and I are the happiest we'll ever be as a couple. We lie low in our dilapidated Southgate flat. We get up late in the short winter days, then in the evening smoke grass and drink red wine long into the night. It's a cool innocent time. We have it all in front of us.

4

New saviour of rock

Late 1992–February 1993. The first Auteurs single, 'Showgirl', released December 1992. Although it sells well it is no match for Whitney Houston, who dominates the US and UK singles charts. On 23 December Funkadelic guitarist Eddie Hazel dies of liver failure at home in New York. In January 1993 the Auteurs headline an NME *show along with riot-grrrl-affiliated-band Cornershop. 'No Limits' by 2 Unlimited is number one in the singles chart for a long time. Suede perform at the Brits. In February more riot grrrl business when Huggy Bear perform 'Her Jazz' on* The Word *TV show, and Pulp release 'Razzamatazz'. At the end of the month the Auteurs debut album* New Wave *enters the UK album charts at 22.*

Tuesday, midday, and in parts of north London you can buy the music weeklies a day early. Tuesday, the day when skinny young things in rock groups nervously scuttle off to the newspaper stands of Kings Cross and Camden Town to read their fate in the lousy prose of the *Melody Maker* and the *NME*. But I have nothing to fear. On the eve of its release in February 1993 *New Wave* is being hailed as a classic by the British music press. For once they've got it right – if you can't come up with the goods on your first album you may as well throw in the towel, Jack. First albums are the result of thousands of ideas germinating throughout those formative years. The crystallisation of hundreds of couplets into fully formed songs. It's a well known adage that you have twenty-odd years to write your first album and then six months to write your second. And so the pile of exemplary notices starts to mount up. Alan Jones, editor of *Melody Maker*, devotes an entire page to his review, comparing my songs to Kinks masterpieces such as 'Two Sisters' and 'End of the Season'. The *NME* follows suit with another full-page review, with their editor Steve Sutherland giving the record 8/10. Oh man, I'm getting the kind of press I could once only have dreamt of. From the very same publications that once ignored the Servants. Of course I bear no grudge.

Contrary to general belief and their own publicity, the 'inkies' never really had a golden age. During the early to mid-70s the *NME* droned on pompously about Genesis, Yes and Jethro Tull to a hairy all-male readership. By late '77 the rag had finally heard the penny drop, desperately grabbing on to the coat-tails of the dying punk movement. At the start of the new decade the *NME* attempted to reinvent itself as the finger-dirtying read of choice for some imagined espresso-sipping, post-punk sophisticate. Unfortunately, the paper lacked the courage of its convictions and refused to jump into the shallow end of the pool and splash about with the *Face* and other such glossy ephemera of the era. In reality, the *NME* in the early 80s was just a whistle-blowing less humorous version of *Socialist Worker*. Christ, even its 'star' writers like Paul Morley were proclaiming Kid Creole and the Coconuts the future of 'New Pop'. New Pop. Hahahaha.

I lie in bed flicking through *Melody Maker*. The cursed *Melody*

Maker,[7] which I happen to be on the front cover of. Pasty-faced and with backlighting for full messianic effect, my hair's too long and – uh oh – I look like Peter Frampton on the sleeve of *Frampton Comes Alive*. Not a good look. The headline reads, 'Last year we brought you Suede, this year we bring you the Auteurs . . .' and in large print, 'THE NEW SAVIOURS OF ROCK'.

Of course I should be overjoyed, skipping through the daisies with a very stupid grin on my face. I've recorded a classic album that has been greeted with ecstatic reviews; I've got money in the bank; and I'm 25 years old – though in interviews I am adding two years on to my real age for gravitas. For one press release I instruct the PR to raise me to a wise old 29. The PR politely demurs. It's just those three words. Saviour. Of. Rock. Have these people heard the album? Saviour of Rock. Why would I want to save rock? The damn thing has been stumbling around like a wounded donkey since 1981. The only thing I want to do with rock is kick the fucker to death and put it out of its misery.

The last three months have been hectic. The Auteurs debut single 'Showgirl' is released at the beginning of December 1992. It picks up excitable press coverage and gets a healthy bit of airplay on the wireless. Hell, the promotional video even makes it on to Saturday morning kids' TV. There's a fair bit of chit-chat about the audacious bar of silence after the first line, 'I took a showgirl for my bride'. It's the best damned moment on the album. Dead air on the radio. Dead air on the TV screen. Dead air on your stereo. John Cage eat your heart out. New saviour of rock, pah. New saviour of silence.

[7] *Melody Maker* has at least by now (1993) lost its jazz and folk sections. In less than a decade it will lose all its sections.

Since the early days of '92 we've picked up an extra member: the Cellist.

'It's beautiful,' says mad Phil, not referring to the music but something else entirely.

'You two both speak the same language,' he continues misguidedly.

Do we? I don't fucking think so, sunshine. Phil Vinall, he must be so perceptive, I ponder, that he can see something profound in my relationship with the Cellist that I cannot. It turns out that Phil is just crazy. But the cello does give us a stately melancholic grace which we would otherwise not possess. The strangest thing that happens with the arrival of the Cellist is that the group no longer feels like a group. Sure, the songs and arrangements had always been down to me, a self-confessed martinet. However, there had always been a camaraderie within the original line-up of Alice, Glenn and myself, a camaraderie born out of struggle, born out of doing this not for the money but because we all know this is a great group. Now we are signed to a major record label there is a fair bit of tacit squabbling about money (tacit, only because the gripes are all relayed to Manager Tony – in confidence – who then sniggeringly relays them back to me). The Cellist, I know, is only here because he is being paid. It's a drag.

We undertake two recording sessions as a four piece prior to the release of the album. On 2 January a BBC session at Maida Vale Studios. People go on and on about the greatness of BBC sessions at Maida Vale – how you're allowed to, like, do anything you want . . . And you're not when you record your own album? Honestly, Maida Vale, it ain't much cop – just a municipal rabbit warren of slightly shabby studios manned forlornly by a handful of clock-on/clock-off engineers. Still the session works out OK and I debut a cool glib song called 'New French Girlfriend'.

The second session a few weeks after the BBC recordings is for potential B-sides. We get to try out our brand new equipment – £10,000 worth. Hut had to drop one of their bands to pay for it. They know we're worth it. I don't feel bad. The fewer groups out there making records the better.

I do however have misgivings about this recording session. I've used up all my songs that were worth recording on *New Wave* and for the 'Showgirl' B-sides. The new songs I have written are too good for B-sides. So I hurriedly 'commission' myself to write especially for the session. Two slow crap songs ('High Diving Horses' and 'Wedding Day') and a prowling third one, 'Lenny Valentino', about the original dirty-mouthed comedian Lenny Bruce taking that final shot of smack in 1966.[8] Instead of mainlining himself straight into heaven, Lenny nods out and finds himself back in old Hollywood at the start of the twentieth century. In his opium reverie the comic finds sanctuary inside Rudi Valentino's body. Unfortunately Valentino has recently died and this is the day of his funeral. The streets of LA are lined with mourners, and from inside the coffin Lenny thinks – in his paranoid dope-addled mind – that they are here to torment him. Even here Lenny Bruce cannot escape his persecutors.

I realise quick smart that this song is no B-side, and Phil Vinall recognises it straight off as a classic. During the lead vocal take I have trouble getting down to a few of the low notes. The Cellist demonstrates that *he* can reach them and kindly offers his services. 'Hey, tough guy, bit keen aren't you?' says Phil to the swot, visibly irritated.

I'm watching you, I think to myself. *I'm watching*.

*

[8] This is the first of many attempts at recording the song.

Early February and Paris is calling me. France is a country where English rock groups traditionally sell jack shit, and so despite all the press attention in the UK weeklies no one at the record company has particularly high expectations. Then something happens. The French press add two and two together and come up with 12. You see the album's called *New Wave* – which translates as *Nouvelle Vague*. The band is called the Auteurs. Auteur theory, *Cahiers du Cinéma*, ah, it all makes sense, a band of English Francophiles. Hell, the singer's name even means Luke Hatred. The second most touted band in Great Britain seem to have French art house leanings. In interviews I am constantly asked if the title of the album refers to a new wave of British bands of which I am at the vanguard.[9] *A new wave of Brit bands all influenced by this Francophile English songwriter?* Well the French wouldn't mind a bit of that.

The Cellist, Manager Tony Beard and I fly to Paris to test the water with an acoustic gig at the Passage Nord Ouest – sadly not the elusive North West Passage beloved of psycho-geographers and Daniel Defoe but a Bohemian venue close to Gard du Nord station. (The low-key acoustic promotional gig is a sure sign that the record company thinks the artist is going to tank, so keep the costs down and that's your lot. Ta very much.) We soundcheck and then go off to tackle a French restaurant. The Cellist reveals himself to be something of a bon viveur in search of an onion pastry called *pissaladière*. As a *non* viveur, I find his quest rather disappointing on any number of levels.

[9] The album title actually derives from a conversation between Go Between Robert Forster and Lawrence from Felt, overheard at a mid-80s party. Forster was the recipient of a berating from Lawrence for wearing purple flared trousers. Lawrence felt that the Go Betweens singer was letting the side down by wearing the offending trousers, which in Lawrence's opinion were 'not new wave'.

There's some kind of movie premiere at a cinema a few hundred yards from the venue and they're queuing round the block for a glimpse of Gerard Depardieu. Then it hits me. The punters aren't here to worship the old French idol; they're queuing to get a glimpse of the new one. *C'est moi*. The tiny 250-capacity venue sold out in minutes. We could have filled it three or four times over. The gig is a revelation. The French existentialists listen in religious reverence. The *New Wave* songs deconstruct perfectly with acoustic guitar and cello. The audience lap it up, surrendering themselves to abandon at the end of each song. Four standing ovations later and I'm back in the dressing room. My good vibes and bonhomie quickly evaporate when I realise there is a dastardly Gallic plot afoot. Within seconds, I'm standing toe to toe and looking down at the top of tiny promoter Dominic's head. Dominic's old pal Guy Chadwick from the House of Love has turned up, and Dominic thinks it would be nice if Chadwick were to play a short impromptu set to my audience, most of whom are still here and drinking at the bar.

'It eez ze way it 'appens in Paris,' offers the French fool. The verbal equivalent of the Gallic shrug.

I'm about to land one on Dominic when Manager Tony steps between us and whisks me off to a toilet cubicle to give me my calming-down pills.

'Dominic is a very powerful promoter. He could be very useful to us.'

Man, I hate all this lickspittle nonsense, but I try and remember this is why I have a manager. I go back and make up with the little French guy. Dominic is all smiles, laughing and joking with me. He knows he's a scamp. He gets his way and poor Guy Chadwick goes onstage. He shouldn't have bothered. It's just one last gasp from a dead man. Chadwick plays his weak psychedelic House of

Love ditties and leaves the stage, his psyche dismantled by the indifference of the crowd, *my* crowd. I smile and shake his hand when he shuffles back into the dressing room. He congratulates me on my amazing performance. I feel no pity towards him. He's yesterday's man. He should be honoured to be in the presence of the new King. Manager Tony and I stumble out of the venue, stoned and giddy with success and possibilities. I run the gauntlet of French fans and drug dealers, who all seem to have a job lot of 'ze good Iranian zmack' that they all want to kindly offload on me. Hmm, maybe they don't like me here so much after all. We finish up in an all-night bar, plotting world domination, wide-eyed and awestruck. We really are getting ahead of ourselves.

Flushed with the success of the Passage Nord Ouest show I head back to Blighty with swollen head (my outward false modesty will soon depart). Within days I am doing a photo shoot in a London studio for French rock bible *Les Inrockuptibles*. The magazine wants to do a joint front cover: Suede's Brett Anderson and me. Naturally we both refuse to share the cover, petulant brats that we are. The magazine bows to the demands of our shared publicists – the painfully hip Best in Press – and does half the print run with me on the cover and the other half with Brett. Inside we both slag each other off furiously safe in the knowledge that the other will not be able to translate. This continues for the next year – respectful and demure about one another in the English music rags while over in the European papers we bitch about each other like a couple of old queens.

Thanks to a moderate – and nifty – record deal Alice and I now have a little money, so the last thing I want to do is go on tour. But, with an album now out, go on tour I must. I'm in this to make records, not to travel around the woebegone provincial shitholes of Great Britain. I am an unreconstructed snob. Even if London has spruced itself up in the early 90s, then the rest of the country looks like it came to a grinding halt some time around the Winter of Discontent. I resent the professionalism creeping into the group, and the constant nagging from certain band members about being put on retainers. Some people, it would seem, have a one-track mind. If they want the money then they're going to have to earn it. I'll expect nothing less than total loyalty. Joylessly, our disharmonious combo undertakes a UK tour to promote *New Wave*. The press adore me and the public come out in force, up and down the country, to listen. Thankfully, I don't let any of this go to my head. The band are brutal and I put out all the bad vibes I can muster to the paying audience, counting off the days until the tour is over.

Tinkle, tinkle. I put down the *Melody Maker* with my face on the front cover, and drag myself out of the hotel bed to answer the blower. These days the phone rings a lot and it's always good news. Still the new girl in town. This time it's Dave Boyd from the record company.

'I hear the tour's going well' says DB with some enthusiasm.

'Well. You know . . .' I answer with somewhat less enthusiasm.

'The album's in at number 22 . . .' At this point I care little and know nothing about chart positions. 'Showgirl' went straight into the independent charts at number one, which to my mind – the mind of an 80s indie veteran – was akin to being in the Eagles.

'Twenty-two . . .' Hmm. 'But didn't "Showgirl" go in at number one?' I shoot back, slightly miffed.

'No, you fucker, 22. Not 22 in the indie album chart, 22 in the grown-up album chart. Well done. Oh, and we've got the album an American release date. You're going to America in April.'

I feel a tinge of excitement.

5

Chocolate Teapot

April–summer 1993. Suede *by Suede goes straight to number one in the UK album charts; it is knocked off the top spot by Bowie's* Black Tie White Noise. *On 29 April* Spider from Mars *guitarist Mick Ronson dies of liver cancer. Also in April* Select *publishes its notorious 'Yanks Go Home' issue, featuring Suede, Auteurs, Denim and Saint Etienne. Blur turn up again in May with their second album* Modern Life Is Rubbish. *It goes top twenty. Mainstream pop is the same as ever, and Take That are number one in the singles chart with something or other. Velvet Underground piss all over their once immaculate reputation by reforming, and the Auteurs play the* NME *stage at Glastonbury.* Gold Against the Soul, *Manic Street Preachers' second album, is released in June.*

At the heart of every doleful Englander there is a big black hole which no amount of privilege can fill. Grace, favour and a perishing wit may temporarily bung it up, but the marauding wanderlust of the island race is merely a distraction from the emptiness within. You can run as far as you like but you will always carry with you an impoverished soul. Only one thing will bring sustenance to that poor soul: empire building. I decide I will start to build my empire by 'breaking America'. This is the mission that my band and I have been sent to complete. We will make audiences happy and they will buy our records by the ton. Our once barren existence will be replenished and our hearts will be filled with joy. Such are my thoughts on landing at New York's JFK Airport for the first time in April 1993. After throwing up with pre-flight nerves I drink my way over the Atlantic. I am a pioneer, so it seems fitting that I wear a First World War aviator hat for the duration of the flight. I pull the leather straps down over my ears so the hat fits tightly over my head. I look like blue comedian Roy 'Chubby' Brown. This is how the Auteurs 'terror campaign' against the world's most powerful nation begins.

Once the enormous hurdle of actually getting aboard the Virgin Atlantic 747 has been surmounted, I realise that I am relieved to be departing Blighty. Since August the previous year we have toured the UK five times – twice supporting Suede and three times on our own. April is the nadir, with a disastrous performance in Sheffield broadcast live on the nation's favourite, Radio 1. Halfway through the show my amp dies, never to be resuscitated. The Cellist covers up brilliantly, doing his best approximation of a John Cale viola panzer attack. Jesus, Radio 1 must have been haemorrhaging listeners.

The gig is merely the culmination of a general wrongness throughout our day in Sheffield. I am supposed to spend the afternoon pre-soundcheck signing copies of *New Wave* in the local Virgin Megastore. This for me stretches the relationship between fan and artist to breaking point, a relationship which I feel ends when the punter hands over the ackers in exchange for the CD. *That* is audience participation and it is sacrosanct. I instead elect to spend my time playing a fruit machine in the bar of the venue. Some lance corporal from the *NME* hovers behind me, taking notes as I pull on the one-armed bandit, scribbling something down as I talk with the road crew. Christ, the man's a pest. I do an interview with the lance corporal, who seems keen to extol the values of what Radio 1 has grandly named Sheffield Sound City. I let slip that I don't care too much for the north and in fact the only thing that interests me about Sheffield is that Peter Sutcliffe had been arrested there in 1981. The *NME* happily prints my northern baiting a few weeks later. The Cellist of course can't get enough of the north. Over the last few months we have been grinding up and down the M1. A gig in Manchester is a homecoming. Leeds, the prodigal son returns. Sheffield, ah, happy childhood memories. Onion tart anyone? The north and the south. Never the twain shall meet.

The other low point of April is the Auteurs' second single 'How Could I Be Wrong?' It's a classic song – a slow graceful funeral march, played by an English Booker T and the MGs and narrated by William Holden in *Sunset Boulevard*. Not a radio hit then. In fact it barely makes a dent on the wireless. Scott Piering, our radio plugger, calls me to suggest a radio remix of the song. I fob him off by pretending he's right. (On this occasion the late great Scott Piering is wrong – no amount of buffing will help 'How Could I Be Wrong?' take over the airwaves.) I don't bother remixing the song and Scott is none the wiser. Phil Vinall, who is spending so much time in the studio that he has lost the power to communicate in the outside world, has been trying his best to forewarn me of the song's radio unworthiness via a series of negative twitches and drunken sighs, but I have been too busy to hear or see him. So the damn thing flops somewhere on the wrong side of the top 75. Fuck it, two months ago the vulgarity of this popularity contest couldn't touch me, but now I'm just like any of the other fuckers. I find I'm in the race to win. Tony calls me with the bad news and some extra sales statistics that the reps (who have to analyse commercial disasters) have kindly provided.

'Well the good news is that the album is selling really well – so you're Led Zeppelin,' he adds improbably for levity, and in part to cushion the blow. 'And the single has sold really well in London, the south and Scotland. Thing is, you've hardly sold any copies in the north of England.'

The north. And the south. And never the twain shall meet.

We touch down in America and clear immigration at JFK with no problem. The humourless immigration officials and the humourless English singer still wearing the aviator hat of the unfunny comedian. My countenance improves on the drive into Manhattan. The first thing that gets you are the signs: Queens, Brooklyn, Rockaway. Ha, it's real; they all exist. *Rock Rock Rockaway Beach*. We are like the many English bands who have come before us (the last place I should be). We are here to, ahem, conquer America. Brett Anderson has been predictably cocky about Suede's US chances, but all the band get for their troubles is stolen equipment and an enforced name change, to the not-much-cop London Suede, after a dust-up with an American singer who goes under the name of Suede. Foretold is forewarned. But not me. I love America. I love Lou Reed. I'm a Coney Island Baby. Soon we'll be in Boston MA. Jonathan Richman's home town.

New York

Alice, Glenn, the Cellist, Mikey the sound man and myself are all deposited outside the Gramercy Park Hotel. Lexington Avenue. New York City looks like – *say it* – Scorsese's 70s. *What's not to love about this country?* Marty Diamond, comedy New Yorker and our American agent, meets us in the lobby. He gives me books as a welcoming gift. New York literature: Jim Carroll's *Forced Entries* is OK, least he's trying, but Eric Bogosian's *Notes from the Underground*. Oh please. Marty is going on and on about 'literate rock 'n' roll' and how he likes to 'walk on the dark side of the street'. Marty Diamond, a little guy who owns a little dog. Two strikes against him in my book, and that's the only book that counts.

As well as fun guy Marty, we pick up two other very bad things in New York. First: Wayne, our brand new American tour manager. With the long dark hair and looks of a male model, Wayne minces around in pristine Levis and Persil-white T-shirt as if he's on the catwalk. I really can't picture this guy lugging heavy gear out of a van. He has just finished tour-managing Radiohead,[10] and improbably comes highly recommended (there are five born every minute). Wayne, from Milwaukee, also has an extremely irritating tick of throwing in faux *zippety do da* phrases every few sentences. The Cellist, who has been to New York before, and boy will he not let us first-timers forget it, has been droning on about finding a good sushi restaurant. Thankfully Wayne has taken a shine to him.

'We gonna get us surm guurd sushi,' he says. Much to my amusement, Mikey, from Blackpool, has taken an instant dislike to our new friend. A shame as they are sharing rooms for the next couple of weeks.

'I hope you ain't got no Aids, boy,' says the paranoid hygiene-obsessed tour manager weirdly and apropos of nothing.

'Well, you never know. Mikey used to drive a forklift on Dover docks,' I say helpfully. We play the requisite couple of shows in Manhattan, the same old shit that every English band, full of blind optimism, before and after will do. CBGB's. Sure, it's a toilet, but

[10] Radiohead have a sizeable hit in America with 'Creep' in late 1993.

remember. I love America. It's CB's, man – Television, Richard Hell, Johnny, Joey, Dee Dee, Tommy – how the fuck can you be cynical about that? So the shows are great and all the cool people on the New York scene come out to see us. Break America? Piece of piss. Then we pick up the second very bad thing: Brenda Khan. Our designated support artist. Myrna Bloody Minkoff.[11]

Boston

As we head off to Boston, Wayne fiddles endlessly with the radio dial.

'You got any Cheap Trick, *boy*?' He asks the radio in his bewildering *Song of the South* accent. Unfortunately the radio has got plenty of Cheap Trick. That old adage about Britain and America being two countries separated by a common language is not strictly true. Same as Americans not understanding irony – they do, and they have a good grasp of sarcasm. The real great cultural divide is the American love of Cheap Trick. I put my aviator hat back on, hoping for even the smallest amount of protection. So with soft rock rattling around my head I steal myself for the long, long drive to Boston. Home of Jonathan Richman and the Modern Lovers, *with the radio on*.

Jonathan Richman and the Modern Lovers. I first heard Richman when I was 15. I pick up a copy of *Rock 'n' Roll with the Modern Lovers* dirt cheap in a second-hand record shop. In Portsmouth in 1982 no one was interested in this kind of record. It doesn't even click with me initially, with its hymns to Boston and a retarded singalong about an ice cream man, but there was somehow enough

[11] Ignatius Reilly's nemesis irritant in John Kennedy Toole's *Confederacy of Dunces*.

there for me to stick with it. A year or so later I get hold of a copy of the seminal *Original Modern Lovers*. This is where it all fell into place. My favourite Velvets albums are the eponymous third album and *Loaded*. Sure, 'Heroin' from the first album is great when you're 13 years old, but it's a relentless and murky solipsistic grind of a song, lacking the uh-huh-uh, white-boy-hanging-with-the-pimps-in-Harlem sass of 'I'm Waiting for the Man'; and 'Sister Ray' is a useful neighbour-hating device, but really life is too short. Give me the sunny nihilistic resignation of 'Oh Sweet Nuthin' any day. Jonathan Richman knew this. A fellow Velvets nut, he took out the dirty-needles-and-hepatitis element of Lou Reed's songs and just kept *that* beat. Boston-born Richman moved to New York in 1969 and hung out with the Factory crowd, scaring the shit out of the freaks in the process and busking his weirdly naive and militant song manifestos around the streets of Manhattan. By the early 70s the Modern Lovers were fully formed and recording classics with John Cale in the producer's chair. The Cale sessions are what make up *The Original Modern Lovers* LP, and this is the one you want – although you may have to get hold of the Kim Fowley-produced sessions, as these contain the only version of 'Don't Let Our Youth Go to Waste'.

And so it begins with 'Roadrunner'. It's the greatest dumbest lyric over the greatest dumbest ripped-off Velvets riff. Richman wrote the damn thing when he was 19 years old. The perfect age for the perfect rock 'n' roll song. 'She Cracked' follows and has everything I love about early Jonathan. A censorious pious lyric over a killer descending Velvets rip (again). Richman sounds like a hectic kind of guy as he castigates some girl for eating 'garbage' and getting stoned while boasting that he stays at home eating health foods. If there's a script for the early 70s he clearly hasn't read it. This is borne out by 'Old World', a celebration of traditional values, loving one's parents and the world they came from. It's an oddly heartbreaking song, and on a good day the lines about 1950s apartment houses and the bleak 70s sun can bring a tear to my eye. 'Astral Plane', 'Girlfriend', 'Someone I Care About' . . . every one of them is a zinger. 'Hospital', with its opening line about being released from hospital – a six-minute begathon where Richman pleads to be let back into the life of a former psychiatric patient. I mean, who the hell writes a song like that? 'Pablo Picasso' is one of several hippy-baiting songs on the album, wherein Jonathan name-calls a longhair on the street 'a bellbottom asshole' while taunting further with the story of the great painter's prowess with the ladies. We learn in the song's most famous lyric that Pablo Picasso was never called an asshole. Unlike the listener to the song.

Best track on *The Original Modern Lovers* is without a doubt 'I'm Straight'. Another militant anti-hippy manifesto in which Jonathan tells the girl on the end of the phone, in his finest asthmatic voice, that 'he's straight' and not stoned like Hippy Johnny. Richman, it transpires, is going to take Hippy Johnny's place. A bold statement in 1973.

As our Auteurs mobile rumbles through Boston I pay tribute by turning off the soft rock and putting *The Modern Lovers Live at the Longbranch Saloon* on the stereo. It's an amateurish affair guaranteed to affront the muso contingent of my band. They sneer as I crank up the truly obnoxious live version of 'I'm Straight' with the amended lyric – Hippy Johnny has now become Hippy Ernie, the unlucky owner of a Woodstock smile and a brain that has been reduced to lysergic mush.

The Modern Lovers disbanded before their debut album came out – as all groups threaten to but never do. Later albums such as the aforementioned *Rock 'n' Roll with . . .*, *Back in Your Life* and *Jonathan Sings!* were recorded with an ever-changing line-up.

Richman had also switched dramatically to a more 'childlike' style of music, and mainly refused to play the old songs. By the 80s Richman had unsurprisingly become a fairly rum fellow. But for *The Original Modern Lovers* and 'I'm Straight' alone I can forgive him pretty much any digressions into the world of *Little Aeroplanes* and *Little Dinosaurs*.

The venue is called the Middle East – it's not a venue, it's a fucking hummus restaurant. We are booked in to play a two night 'residency'.

'Do you guys wanna go on last?' says Brenda Khan, Jewish princess, generic Greenwich Village folk throwback and support 'artiste'. Khan has been put on the tour via some collusion between Marty Diamond and her label Sony Records. In other words the only person to lose out is going to be me.

'Yeah, seeing as we are advertised as the headline act I thought we would go on last. That OK with you?' I add sweetly.

'Cool,' she shoots back, unruffled.

Brenda is giving it the big New York I Am act, her Bohemian rich girl shtick designed to rub me up the wrong way, so I make my excuses and go downstairs to the 'venue', where Mikey is breaking out in a sweat.

'Where's Wayne?' I ask.

'You mean Choco,' says Mikey. 'He disappeared as soon as the van needed unpacking.'

'Why Choco?'

'Cos he's about as useful as a chocolate fucking teapot.'

The Chocolate Teapot and I have had a disagreement. He refuses to do any lugging of gear because he is the tour manager, and that is all he will do, manage the tour – 'It's a union thing.' The first night at the Middle East went well. As in Paris, the Bohemians were out in force, looking like extras from the Tony Hancock film *The Rebel*. Brenda Khan's set went on and on – presumably because she thought that if she couldn't headline she'd just play through the headliners' time slot until she was forcibly removed. Tonight, the second night of our residency, I have attempted to miss as much of her set as possible. I arrive back at the venue with only minutes to spare before going onstage. Jesus Christ, she's still at it and torturing the dwindling audience with a dead dog of a song called 'Grout'. On and on it goes. 'Grout! Grout!' screams the banshee over her tuneless guitar. *Grout! Grout!* What is she going on about, retiling her bathroom? Or perhaps Harry Grout, the King Rat of Slade Prison in the popular 70s television comedy *Porridge*, played by the excellent character actor Peter Vaughn.

By the time we leave Boston the next morning, a few changes have been made. Firstly, I throw Brenda Khan off the tour. I phone Marty Diamond to tell him the good news.

'It's all rock 'n' roll,' shrugs comedy Marty, a little dog yapping away in the background.

Brooklyn Brenda does keep in touch though, kindly sending a photograph of herself taking a dump on to the next venue.

The second change concerns our mode of transport. None of us can stand to be in the tour bus with Choco and his soft-rock tyranny, so we have hired an Oldsmobile to take us to the next gig in Washington DC. The five of us squeeze into the family car and enjoy a Cheap Trick-less journey, safe in the knowledge that Choco is driving on ahead, singing along to 'I Want You to Want Me' alone in the tour bus with only a pile of equipment for company. Equipment that he cannot touch. Union regulations.

Chicago

'I've spiked your drummer,' says the maniac. I'm halfway through reading Ed Sanders' account of the Tate–La Bianca murders and notice that the guy talking to me is a dead ringer for Manson Family member Tex Watson. 'The dude's in pieces; I've totally taken him apart.'

Glenn Collins, the dude in question, has had his drink spiked by Tex. He has just returned from the parking lot at the back of a 'sports bar' – the venue for the Chicago gig – where to round things off he has shared a joint of super-strong American weed with our crazy new friend. Before I get the chance to pull Tex up on the moral dubiousness of psychologically wrecking my drummer, the madman gets in first with an offer of a threesome with his girlfriend, who has just announced that she is a vampire. That's me, Tex and the vamp. I give the offer some careful thought but politely decline, gesturing to Alice across the room.

'It's cool. We can party as a foursome, man,' says Tex.

In the family car, on the way back to the hotel, it is clear that Glenn has been 'totally taken apart'. Trouble is, the dude's quite annoying with it. There's nothing left to do but have some fun. I tear some eyeholes in a white paper bag and put it over my head. I transport the tripping drummer back to the Deep South of the 1930s, where a kangaroo court is taking place and Glenn Collins is on trial for his life.

I eventually put Glenn safely to bed, assuring him he won't be hanged tomorrow, and then head down to the hotel bar. 'Tex Watson's' freaky madness seems to have adversely affected us all. Never meet your audience, however much they might want to meet you. Outside, a storm rages. The television over the bar blares out severe weather warnings and doomy news about planes bobbing about in the sky, stranded in holding patterns, unable to land at O' Hare Airport. Tomorrow we fly to San Francisco. Everyone's hitting the cocktails hard and it's starting to get ugly so I head back to my room. On the flickering TV a news story cuts into the apocalyptic weather transmission. There's another kind of Armageddon taking place in Texas. I stay up into the night and watch the Waco siege unfold. God, I love America. I just hope that Glenn's not watching.

San Francisco

'What's San Francisco like?' replies Mikey, shooting back my rather broad question. 'It's a right fucking roughhouse town – that's what it's like.'

Mikey's reply is approximately the third thing on my mind as I am pinned to the floor of the Phoenix Hotel. The Phoenix Hotel in San Francisco's less than salubrious Tenderloin district, an oasis of rock 'n' roll surrounded by a nightmare vision of dawn-of-the-dead junkies slowly lurching toward the stray tourists, who have taken the wrong turning out of the financial zone into this cesspit of all humanity, where life's truly hopeless lie in wait for them. Tenderloin. It's not the first time that a couple of the walking dead have got into the hotel. One of them holds me down with a knife at my throat as his undead pal rifles the inside pocket of my leather coat. The second thing on my mind is: *Why me? Why not the English journalist who came over here to write a feature for one of the monthlies? Surely he would have been so cash-light they would have killed the fucker*. It's the tour float I cajoled from Choco that saves me. I'm rich pickings and the job is done quickly and efficiently. I'm left on the floor, shaken and disturbed.

The following morning we walk up Haight Street for more

dawn-of-the-dead fun. Mikey's right, this is a roughhouse town. The detritus of the Summer of Love – the real manic street preachers – confirms that the counterculture was not entirely a good thing. I head back to the hated hotel to try and pull myself together for the show.

As I was had last night, I decide that tonight I will be taking a trophy: Choco's head. The venue, an actual venue, not a restaurant or a sports bar, is rammed. I have set the hapless tour manager an impossible task – impossible for him to carry out to my satisfaction at least – to restring my old Hofner guitar. An unwieldy beast, especially if you have never changed a set of guitar strings before. I bound up the stairs to the dressing room, summoning all the bad vibes that San Francisco has to offer me. There he sits, in that spotless white T-shirt balancing my guitar on his perfect Levi's. He's even got himself a couple of rock chicks that he's trying to impress with that idiotic faux Southern accent. *Faaantastic*. He's made a pig's ear of the string change. I stare him down. The rock chicks have stopped yapping and can sense something's up. Mikey, seated ringside, enjoying the show.

'What the fuck are you doing?' I gesture towards my stricken axe. Without allowing him to answer. 'You are one of the laziest cunts I've ever met. Now fuck off out of my dressing room. I never want to see you again. You're fucking sacked.'

I hold the door open for the confused Choco and watch his male-model hair swish down the stairs. Of course it was a token sacking as we only have a couple of dates to go until the end of the tour. After the evening's blistering show, I get a phone call from Marty D. He's been fielding calls from an angry Chocolate Teapot. I get in there first: 'It's all rock 'n' roll, Marty.'

Los Angeles

So, minus Choco the tour manager, we land at LAX Airport . . . then go into freefall. We fritter away what's left of the already depleted tour float on hiring expensive sports cars to race around Beverly Hills. We play two storming sell-out gigs at the legendary Whisky a Go Go. Scenesters and record execs come out in force.

'Just like seeing the Kinks in '68' says LA hipster Danny Benair.

God, I'm good, I reflect, only just managing to keep this insight to myself. Before this American jaunt, Manager Tony had heard that the Kinks (of '93) want us to support them on their US comeback tour. I am eagerly awaiting confirmation of this anytime soon. Now that the final meet and greet is over there's nothing to do but hang around in the Hyatt Hotel, hoping to catch a glimpse of Little Richard (who lives on the fifth floor) and wait for the flight back to London.

The phone rings in my room. Manager Tony sardonically congratulates me on completing the tour. When he starts off with lukewarm bonhomie I know he's about to throw in a curve ball. Sure enough. 'Sony (the Kinks' record company) are not very happy about their artist Brenda Khan being thrown off the tour. They don't want you on the Kinks tour.'

- One sacked support artist
- One sacked tour manager
- One missing tour float
- One mugged singer
- One lost Kinks tour

America then. Undoing of cocky Brit bands, heads swollen with the overblown praise of the *NME*. America can provide a sobering shot of reality.

We return to the United Kingdom, where we will spend the summer doing festivals and then touring France. The world's most powerful nation remains resolutely unbroken. 'It's all rock 'n' roll,' as fun guy Marty would say.

6

Done up like a kipper

September 1993. The following albums have been nominated for the Mercury Music Prize: Apache Indian – No Reservations, *Gavin Bryars* – Jesus Blood Never Failed Me Yet, *Dina Carroll* – So Close, *PJ Harvey* – Rid Of Me, *New Order* – Republic, *Stereo MCs* – Connected, *Sting* – Ten Summoner's Tales, *Suede* – Suede, *Stan Tracey* – Portraits Plus *and the Auteurs* – New Wave. *The UK number one album is something called* Music Box *by Mariah Carey.*

Accident and Emergency, University of London College Hospital

Wednesday, 16 September 1993. 1.25 a.m. Waiting time: two to three hours. I had a maxim throughout the 90s that it wasn't a good night out unless it ended in A & E. It had been a good night out. Brickies, carpenters, common-or-garden drunks (from which I of course excluded myself) and the luckless and the lucky. I was grimly proud of my night's work. Putting my fist through a glass panel in the private VIP suite of Grosvenor House had been the perfect end to a wretched evening. It was an urge that up until now I have been able to resist. That same urge I have in a recording studio – to douse the multitrack tape machine in wine or hack at the magnetic tape with the editing razor. Weeks of pressing PLAY and RECORD in an attempt to capture the magic, all ruined, just because I can. The hand injury is not serious. Bloody, but no severed tendons. A few tiny shards of glass to be removed just below and above the knuckle of the index and middle fingers of my right hand. Always too near the knuckle. I had evidently not done the job properly. A few stitches and, no doubt, a bill for the damage. I get off lightly. It would not always be the way. At least the blood and action wiped the smile off the face of that lackey from the Mercury committee, one of life's lance corporals if ever there was, with whom, I feel, I have queered my pitch somewhat. I do not expect an invite back. (I see the lance corporal a year or so later at a TV recording. Sadly the obsequious smile has returned.) Waiting time. It had been a good night.

I am already drunk by the time I arrive at Grosvenor House, which is a good start as it is my intention to get colossally drunk this evening. Our party consists of myself, Alice, Glenn, Phil Vinall, the Cellist and manager Tony Beard.

New Wave has been nominated, along with nine other albums, for the 1993 Mercury Music Prize – only in its second year, and already a feeble-minded sports day for the music biz. A 25-grand booty for the winner and forests of publicity for the ten nominees. This is all supposed to translate into that record company Holy Grail: sales.

The Mercury nomination had kept me going through the long summer festival season. Indeed, I first heard of our inclusion on the shortlist while standing in a grey muddy field in Denmark. But now the evening of the award has arrived, other thoughts are whirring across my brain. I cast my mind back to the start of the year. A line from that *NME* review of the album, about me being 'too much of an outsider looking in . . .' Fuck it, the *NME* was almost right. I *am* an outsider looking in. Though it's not quite as simplistic as they would have us believe. I am a practitioner of high art. High art in a low-art medium. I am at best ambivalent about all this Mercury malarkey. You see, I know the record is a work of genius. In this matter I am untroubled by doubt and quite frankly a little niggled that a panel of judges have to debate this. Surely this says more about their own limited critical faculties. I am certain that no person here is qualified to give me this accolade. I curse these Mercury swine. What do they know about art when they reduce everything into a competition to win a medal from a poxy phone company? It's an unfortunate epiphany to have just had, and the timing could have been better. So, with bad vibes rattling round my head, I disembark from my taxi and stumble into a champagne reception for the 1993 Mercury Music Prize. Miffed.

Grosvenor House on Park Lane has, for tonight, transformed itself into a Mecca for the delusional and mediocre. A trough from which they will fill their yapping holes with caviar and lobster. A bucket from which they will guzzle Moët et Chandon, gratis. A cistern from which they can snort cocaine cut with sulphuric acid and laxative into their empty viscous snapping brains. I have flaunted the dress code and opted for an off-beige slightly soiled 'flasher' mac. Tonight, I am debuting my avant-garde pornographer look. It is the least I can do.

Our little party is ushered off to its designated table where I will eat my last meal as the condemned man. A man who is about to be executed at the altar of light entertainment. My jailers for the evening are Dave Boyd and John Best, a PR man whose company

Best in Press will come to represent everything – *whisper it* – Britpop. John Best and his partner Phil Savidge may both be smart men of otherwise impeccable taste, but a joke's a joke, guys, and come Judgement Day these two will have to stand trial for their involvement in the atrocities of the age. Atrocities that will include trying to foist such utter tommyrot as Powder, Marion, Menswear and Echobelly onto a weak and effete nation.

When the Mercury's shortlist was announced back in July, David Boyd had taken me aside and told me, 'You shouldn't underestimate how much power you wield at Virgin Records.' *Woah, Dave. Easy, tiger*. Big mistake. That was not a good piece of information to pass on to someone with such a highly developed sense of self. I intuitively decide to misuse DB's indiscretion by picking a fight. I make some starry speech telling David Boyd how my attendance at the Mercury will compromise my artistic integrity. Of course it's all bullshit. Boyd thinks it's affectation; he knows that acting dead modest just ain't my style. Weeks go by and I remain intransigent. It's gonna be a no-show, baby. Forty-eight hours before the big day and Boyd's frustration with my awkwardness is boiling over. We are at phone-slamming-down loggerheads. But then the bastard calls my bluff by saying that if I don't attend then neither will he. It's a classic potlatch.[12] Oh man, there can only be room for one prima donna. If you don't go, Dave, then my grand gesture will have been for nothing. Still, we are both here now so there's

[12] Potlatch has been described as 'the offering of non-saleable gifts'. It occurred in some North American Indian tribes of the late nineteenth century. The tribes had an unusual practice. One chief met another tribe's chief and offered gifts. The second chief had to reciprocate on a higher plane of value. The game might begin with the presentation of beads and end with a tribe burning down its own village.

nothing to do but kiss and make up. Dave Boyd – gotta love him. Years later, after Hut Recordings have haemorrhaged half a dozen jackpot rollovers of cash, David counsels me with the line 'I didn't sign you to sell records.' Wonderful.

Shithouse. Our table is only ten yards from the stage. This means we might really be contenders to win the damned thing. (Our closing odds from William Hill are 10–1.) But then, five yards, smack bang in front of centre stage is the Suede table. In prime position for the waiting photographers. The press have attempted to set us and Suede up as some sort of vanguard for what they will laughably insist is called Britpop. No dice. The Auteurs are European, intense and intellectual. Suede are a quick fix. Baked beans and sulphate. Brett's pseudo-bumboy androgyny is more *Grange Hill* than Bowie. There is an irrational voice in my head telling me we might win. I must quash it with alcohol. But no, the voice is strong. Perhaps I can strike a blow for outsider art . . . Oh you poor, poor, deluded fool.

I wander off before the ceremony begins to look for trouble. The usual long queues for the cubicles. In the corridors of the Grosvenor Peter Hook from New Order apprehends me.

'Oi, you fookin' cheeky cunt.' He lunges at me. Hooky now has me in a headlock. It's OK. I think it's affectionate. I met him a few months ago. I think Hooky is using the headlock as an esoteric way of imparting ancient knowledge to me. He is trying to say, 'Look, neither of us really belongs here, so stop being so uptight and enjoy yourself.' Hooky's probably right, I think to myself, as the one-time bass player from Joy Division loosens his grip on my head.

'My warmest congratulations on making the shortlist.' A hand reaches out to shake mine. The hand extends from inside a luminous green boiler suit. A boiler suit with preposterous shoulder pads.

The owner of the boiler suit is God's Own Nitwit: Sting. A man who has scratched and clawed his way to the top using only the sheer power of his ambition, cunningly tossing aside any foolish notions of sense or integrity. He has achieved all this so he can stand before me tonight, magnanimously bestowing on me his holy blessing. They're all at it. Thank you, Sting. Behind him, Peter Hook sniggers and gurns like a naughty schoolboy.

It feels like it goes on for hours and hours. Each nominee has had an awful video blurb made about them. The lance corporal from the Mercury committee does a little presentation for each one, his corporate bonhomie grating a little more each time. Our video blurb was shot a few weeks ago. I was so affronted with the whole treatment and the fact I hadn't been consulted that I spend the entire filming walking out of shot. Now, seeing myself up on the big screen, I have to say I am rather pleased with the results. My obstreperousness has given the film a far more avant-garde feel than it would otherwise have had. Excellent. A few people clap. Finally we get to what everyone has being waiting for. Everyone but me.

Suede. They give the prize to Suede. These things happen so quickly. It's like that old news footage of the Viet Cong carrying out executions. Just a dull thud from the gun, a bullet in the back of the head, and a body flopping silently into a ditch.

Cameras catch our reactions. The Cellist's is vocal and demonstrative: 'It's a fucking fix!' bellows the classically trained wage earner, who then follows up with the continental underarm 'Up yours' gesture.

It would be funny if it had been delivered by someone cool. Especially as his ungracious turn has been fleetingly caught by the BBC News cameras. The rank and file misbehaving. Probably only upset that he's not up for a payout tonight. It's like losing some six-a-side park kickabout for him. By the time he gets home and changes out of his demob suit, he won't care. John Best also does the press for Suede. Jesus Christ, I have never seen a man move so fast. One minute he is on our table, the next he is perched on the winning one. John Best, honorary Spider from Mars, moves like a tiger on Vaseline. A female *Guardian* journalist from the judging panel sits down next to me.

'If it makes you feel any better,' says the journalist, 'you only lost by one vote.' *Of course it doesn't make me feel any better, you fucking moron*. Brett Anderson is up on the podium making some idiotic speech about how Suede are pariahs, persecuted by the music industry, and how everybody in the room tonight hates them. What a plank. He's right on the third count though.

Alice looks over at me with sympathy. She realises it before I do. I really am taking this quite badly. People want me to take it badly. This time I oblige. I try and congratulate various members of Suede: Matt Osman then drummer Simon Gilbert. A real sweetie. What I mean to say is 'Well done.' What I actually say is 'Give me my fucking money now.' With menace. Thankfully Simon is wise and knows there is no point in engaging with a wounded drunk.[13] Tomorrow, when I am literally and metaphorically receiving the bill for the evening's debacle, I will wish I had remembered the G.K. Chesterton quote, 'a true gentleman is never unintentionally offensive'. Phil Vinall, who perhaps has remembered his Chesterton, is off on one. Needling various members of New Order. I take my foot off the brakes. I can feel the roller coaster shift downwards.

[13] In Suede's acceptance speech the winners announce that they will give the prize money to a cancer charity. In the fog of defeat I miss this. The prize money has remained at £20,000 since 1992. They clearly haven't heard of inflation.

One problem has been solved. I know that I have to sack Glenn Collins. My loyal friend and drummer. He's been there from the start because he loves my songs. Sure, the money has helped and he now gets attention from ladies who normally wouldn't look at him. But he's a fragile sort, and a year of constant touring has taken its toll. His drumming style is at best primitive, untutored and very cool. No frills and no fills. Unfortunately he's erratic as well. Sometimes songs end abruptly onstage, and I turn around to glare at a bemused hurt-looking drummer who's wondering why the rest of the band are carrying on into the next verse without him. His lack of technique and my constant haranguing have caused a repetitive strain injury in his wrists. We are due to tour France in November and soon after that start recording the second album. It's miserable, but I know I cannot carry him any longer. I know it and he knows it. Losing tonight's gong means I no longer have a moral quandary: I no longer have to share the prize money – that I haven't won – with a drummer who is about to be sacked. This award ceremony is really bringing out the best in me.

Brett Anderson is in the foyer lolling over an opulent Steinway he cannot play. He fingers the piano keys in what he presumes to be a detached wasted manner. He is of course completely aware of the small crowd he is drawing. The lance corporal from the Mercury committee looks at him lovingly. His boy. This is what it has all been for. He is satisfied with his work. I try and evade the lepers, but the Mercury man has already caught my eye. The remains of our party – Manager Tony, Vinall (having narrowly avoided a Mancunian pasting), Alice, Glenn and I are led upstairs to a private suite in the Grosvenor. It's the usual bullshit. Cocaine, champagne. More cocaine, more champagne. I fall into a table of glasses generously filled with Perrier Jouët. I have achieved optimum inebriation and am acting like a peasant. Alice is trying to coax me out of the suite. Even Vinall, in his advanced state, knows I am falling apart. The lance corporal makes one final obsequious remark and I let fly. Haymaker. *Unlucky, sunshine*. I am too drunk to connect. Instead my fist goes through a glass panel about three feet wide of my intended target.

Waiting time two to three hours. It has been a good night out.

7

Brick budgie

October 1993. Nirvana's final studio album In Utero *is knocked off the number one position by the Pet Shop Boys'* Very, *which in turn is deposed by an album by Take That. After the previous month's Mercury Music Prize, there is no marked increase in sales of the Auteurs'* New Wave.

Say it under your breath, whisper it if you can bear to. *Britpop*. Now, if you can, dare to say it out loud: BRITPOP. The final insurrection of the twentieth century. The century of Dada, the Surrealists, Italian Futurism, Russian Futurism, *The Rite Of Spring*, Wyndham Lewis, *Blast*, William Burroughs, the Beats, Gene Vincent, Pablo Picasso, Johnny Kidd and the Pirates, Viennese Actionists, Nijinsky, the Merry Pranksters, Brian Clough, Aleister Crowley, Stanley Spencer, Kenneth Anger, the Stones, King Tubby's, Jean Luc Goddard, Fritz Lang, Burton and Taylor, Andy Warhol Superstars, the Factory, Valerie Solanas, *The Scum Manifesto*, Kendo Nagasaki, the Red Army Faction, Ingmar Bergman, Karl Heinz Stockhausen, Chuck Berry, Timothy Leary, Lettrism, Alfred Hitchcock, the Situationist International, Sly and the Family Stone, the Japanese Red Army, Lord Lucan, Gustav Metzger, Lou Reed, Big Youth, Teddy Boys, T. Rex, Howard Devoto, Bo Diddley, *Performance*, Colin Wilson, the Doors, Punk Rock, Poly Styrene, and now, the last great millennial hurrah, *Britpop*. Scream it from the pit of your fucking stomach till you can scream no more. Thought not.

I am none of the following, but have been described variously as: the pioneer of, the godfather of, the man who invented, the butcher of, and the forgotten man of Britpop (1990s version). Let's not get too bogged down in tracing the lineage any further back. It's never cost-effective and always leads back to a caveman banging a rock with the tusk of a woolly mammoth.

A Fairy Tale

Once upon a time, in the faraway land of Britannia, there were two popular singing groups. The first group was called Suede; they were the more popular of the two singing groups. All the little girls and boys of the kingdom of Britannia loved the Suede group and their singer called Brett. He sang songs to them of his life lived in council houses and sniffing glue, and when he sang he swished his floppy hair around and pulled funny faces. All the children laughed and danced and swooned. The other group was called the Auteurs. They were not as popular as the Suede group, although they had better songs. One of these songs was called 'American Guitars'. Some of the lance corporals of the kingdom of Britannia thought they heard a story in the song about an ancient mythical war between Britannia and the old kingdom of America. In their excitement the lance corporals hadn't listened to the words of the song properly. Nevertheless, it gave them an idea about a new kind of music for the children of Britannia. They announced their idea in *Select* magazine in April 1993. On the cover of the magazine the singer called Brett pulled one of his funny faces in front of the stripy flag of Britannia. The lance corporals had written the commandment 'Yanks Go Home' in crayon above the popular singer's funny face. Inside, the less popular singer from the Auteurs said some things about the kingdom of Britannia, as did some older groups with names like Saint Etienne and Denim. The lance corporals realised that the children of Britannia were never going to love the two older groups so they banished them from the kingdom. What they really needed were lots more younger groups like Suede and the Auteurs to sing to the children of Britannia.

But over in the old kingdom of America there was an ogre, an ogre that could not be banished, for he was too talented and blessed with the evangelical primal spirit of rock 'n' roll through the ages. All the children of the whole world loved Kurt the ogre, for he was kind and gentle. However, the lance corporals knew that Kurt was depressed and addicted to heroin, and were sure that one day he would take his own life. It would only be after that sad day that the lance corporals would be allowed to unleash their new music for the children of Britannia: they would call it Britpop.

October 1993, just days before my 26th birthday. Although Britpop may be creep-crawling my room when I sleep, I have a pressing engagement on my mind. I have to sack Glenn Collins. It's been lingering for months, and now after the Mercury Music Prize 'defeat' the time is as right as it is ever going to be for pissing on the drummer's chips. Was it right to carry Glenn this far? To build up his hopes? Is it right that I already have a replacement drummer in place? I curse my vague answers when Glenn asks me about the forthcoming European tour – which he will be excluded from – and *When are we going to start recording the new album?* So we meet up on a Saturday night in a boozer in Crouch End and I do the deed. Glenn sees the assassin's bullet heading straight between his eyes in slow motion. We shake hands and he takes it like a man. Miserable stuff. Trouble is, Glenn always wanted to be popular, and he rightly senses that something is afoot – Suede, Auteurs, Pulp, someone is trying to take this somewhere. He thinks his chance has gone, that he has been thrown off the boat just as it's leaving the harbour. Glenn need not have worried.

8

Adolf Hitler of Britpop

November 1993. Pulp release 'Intro' on Island Records. Elastica release their first single, 'Stutter'. Throughout November and the beginning of December Meatloaf is number one in the UK singles chart. Just to consolidate the awfulness of their reunion, The Velvet Underground release a live album.

Armistice Day. 'Lenny Valentino', a song the record company had originally deemed too 'art' to be a single, has been A-listed by Radio 1.

'If you want us to release this as an art statement then we will,' says Dave Boyd at the record company meeting. 'But you've got to decide whether you're making an art statement or a commercial statement,' says Pontius Pilate. The song is one hundred and twenty seconds of meta-Motown-Dada genius. So it must be a commercial art statement – if you can't say it in two minutes then don't say it at all. Meanwhile, the schedule has gone into overdrive. After two days of hurried rehearsal I have knocked together a live set with our new powerhouse of a drummer: Barney

C. Rockford. A chiselled, stoned surfer. Ladies love him; everybody likes him. In this group Barney C. Rockford is incongruous to say the least.

The Auteurs, Pulp and the Boo Radleys have been booked to play a four-night travelling festival in France organised by French rock rag *Les Inrockuptibles*. The shows are our biggest to date, and as usual I am glad to be leaving the old country. I'm not playing the game with the English music press, laughing at their silly scene-making; I'm haughtily slagging off every new group that comes along. I think I may be turning into a pariah. I have a romantic vision of an exiled maverick – Isherwood in Berlin or a character from a Graham Greene novel – cast out by his fellow countrymen into the welcoming arms of the old enemy. The dirty collaborators of the Vichy government. The hated French.

We board a slow ferry to Calais with Pulp, who over the last six months have been getting good. Their last single 'Razzamatazz' was a classic. Even though I was unhappy that *our* producer Phil Vinall had worked with them, I had to concede to the song's audacious charm. Happily, Pulp's new single 'Lipgloss' – to be released the same week as 'Lenny Valentino' – is piss-poor, a weedy unfocused mess with a botched production by Suede producer *de jour*, Ed Buller. This temporary state of one-upmanship gives me carte blanche to spread my appalling bonhomie over various Pulp members, as I knock back early-morning red wine from the ship's bar and ponce about on deck in my extravagantly awful three-quarter-length beige corduroy car coat. The conquering hero, returning to his loyal citizens.

Jarvis and I make awkward conversation. We already have form together as veterans of the Fire label, but I can't quite shake the image of him as a spear-chucking, loincloth-wearing assassin from my strange dream about Clive Solomon. Pulp's career has run like one of those silent movies showing man's early attempts at aviation. Each Pulp release is like a preposterous flying machine trundling toward the cliff edge, only to break up like balsa wood as it flops into the sea. Now Jarvis has his pilot's licence, he's packed up his amateur birdman wings and has one eye on Woolworths. In a few years' time he will even have the gall to coquettishly wonder how he became Jarvis, Man of the People, loved by all. The Queen Mother of Pop. Pleasingly, I seem to have upset Pulp's drummer Nick Banks (along with most northern music press readers) with my cheerful anti-northern quips recently printed in the *NME*. Happy with my morning's work, I wander up to the top deck of the ship. I need to figure out a plan of escape. Refuge from the long van journey ahead down to the south of France. Sanctuary from the endless excitable twittering about how *On the next tour we will be so professional that we will probably be able to afford a sleeper bus*. God help you all.

I am sitting in the ship's forlorn cinema with Russel Senior, Pulp's guitar 'n' violin botherer. Up on the big screen old Hanna-Barbera cartoons flicker away. With the recent arrival of our new drummer – an enthusiast of altered reality – I find that many things that were off the menu are now back on. So to ease my worsening travel neuroses I neck two Mogadons. The red wine is also starting to kick in. Russell is dressed like a thrift-store Italian fascist. (Soon the great Scottish songwriter Momus will refer to me as the Adolf Hitler of Britpop. It's a comparison perhaps more suited to Damon Albarn. If anything at all, I am more Albert Speer.) Next cartoon up is one of my childhood favourites, *Help! It's the Hair Bear Bunch*. Yeah, this lot have got it sussed. Each member of the bunch acts as a counterpoint to another and this synthesis means that their Mr Peavly-baiting antics run like a precision piece of machinery. A perfect rock 'n' roll group living in Cave Block No. 9 at the

Wonderland Zoo. I can tell that Russell is content just to be breathing the same air as his favourite songwriter. Man, it is such a drag. Russell should be in my band, then at least we would be a real group. Since the addition of Barney C. Rockford we have become a powerfully dynamic live unit, but the problem is that I am now in all but name a singer/songwriter touring with my girlfriend and a couple of hired hands. A decade later and Russell Senior tells me that around this time he was going to offer me his services as a manager – or stylist, whichever I felt I needed more. Lucky escape.

After 12 hours submerged, I begin to resurface from the deep. Our splitter bus – road crew in the front, band in the middle, equipment in the back – has hit Marseilles. I know I'm in a bad way when I see white horses being walked around the first floor of a large tenement block. Alice reassures me it is no hallucination and that I do not require rethreading. Not yet anyway. We are of course back in France, and we have merely witnessed a beautiful old-fashioned slaughterhouse operating in full view of the public highway.

Support acts are a drag. Being the support act and, if you are the headliner, tolerating the support act – all a huge fucking drag. I have come to this entirely unreasonable and impractical conclusion after our last tour of France back in the summer. The record label has decided to saddle us with their new signing, David Gray, as the opening act. Gray turns out to be a pseudo-Welsh mentalist, pissing off our audience with his dreary, never-ending, sub-Roy-Harper dirges. Between numbers the folkie goes off on one, with Tourette's-like bouts of 'Oggie oggie oggie' rabble-rousing (leaving the French crowds utterly mystified). Gray also has a nasty tick for lengthy onstage guitar-tuning sessions. *Deoowwwing*. String goes down. *Boowwang*. String goes up. Time passes, somewhere a life flickers out, and somewhere a new life begins. Yeah, strum a chord, see if it sounds OK. *Murwaaang!* No improvement then. Christ, there's no let-up. Offstage he's not much better, diving into swimming pools fully clothed. Losing his hotel room keys and having to break in through a window. I have an immediate reaction to attention-seekers – to give them none. Gray believes the hype – thinks I'm some haughty aristo who looks down on him. He's only two-thirds right, but it's OK, I'm not looking for friendship. I didn't think it could get worse than Gray. I have a lot to learn. Tonight we are sharing the bill with the Boo Radleys.

Rock critics habitually throw around references to 70s dub, Brian Wilson and Scott Walker like bullets at a high-school massacre. It's OK, they don't really mean it. These are just the kind of artists they would prefer to be writing about, as opposed to the ones that they have to write about. Enter the Boo Radleys. 'Sharing the bill' means we take it in turns to headline. Tonight, the Boos go on last.

Martin Carr is the Boo Radleys' resident 'genius'. He is the lucky recipient of the kind of hyperbolic prose I was getting nine months earlier. His band are currently touring an abomination of an album called *Giant Steps*. It features all the predictable *TSB* Rock School dub and inept approximations of Miles Davis. In two years' time the Boo Radleys will do the unthinkable and make a record that is actually worse than *Giant Steps*. A record that even King Dunce Alan McGee (their label boss) will disown. The record is called *Wake Up Boo*: three words guaranteed to induce nausea and a cold sweat, followed by the kind of killing spree that will forever be preceded by the phrase 'tragic events'.

Marseilles is my kind of town. Fractious, intolerant and right wing. Algerian drug dealers rub up against the Riviera well-to-dos and the hoi polloi. I am lost in a megalomaniacal reverie as we enter the venue for tonight's show. I snap out of it sharpish as I am introduced to the promoter, a bastard South African who insinuates that he will take my record off the club's playlist if I don't do this or do that. And I thought corruption only existed in the corridors of power.

I take the stairs to our shared dressing room to find three bodies writhing in the doorway. I accidentally tread on some hair and a Scouser squeals. The hair and squeal belong to a Boo Radley, engaging in their customary roughhousing. This lot seem to be pathologically incapable of setting foot outside their windowless tour bus without breaking into a bout of rough and tumble with one another. The bodies pick themselves up from the deck.

'Awlrigh', mate?' an exaggerated Mersey accent enquires, leering toward me. The implication seems to be of the *Do you want some?* variety. Hmmm, the backstage drinks rider is already seriously depleted. *Are you really trying to menace me?* I wonder. I hold out my hand and offer my finest limp-wristed handshake and my most sickly simpering smile. The north. The south. And never the twain shall meet. All friends then.

Ce soir, je suis magnifique. And the band is pretty damned good too. Live, Rockford can drive songs to the point of combustion. 'Modern History', a new song that started out as a stately acoustic ballad on the American tour, has now turned into an epic, with a laughing clowns playout. The Cellist even imitates Steven Mackay's 'Fun House' sax squawks. To wrap up the show I give the audience a blast of 'La Marseillaise', followed by a sarky '*Vive la France*' and a Benny Hill salute. They lap it up, won't let us go, so I play one extra encore. Just enough to cut into the Boo Radleys' set time, having learnt well from Brooklyn Brenda. Of course the Scousers are too drunk to notice. I've taken a gamble that by the time we get to Paris – when I will be headlining – they won't try and pull the same underhand trick on me. The promoter, however, has noticed, and is not so happy about my onstage mock-French-nationalism. They're a sensitive lot down here. Predictably, he tries to squirm out of paying us our agreed fee. This is all nonsense and will eventually be resolved by Big Neil, our tour manager. I decide to leave them to it and wander out into the Marseilles night with Rockford in search of opium.

En route to Paris. The road crew are worried about the French motorway police. In recent months they have started pulling over all foreign vans. That is, vans that look like rock 'n' roll tour buses. It's a no-brainer. A rumour is in circulation that if any illicit substances are recovered then there will be a heavy on-the-spot fine. Threats of jail are no longer made. It's a complicit agreement. Sure enough we are pulled over several hours into our journey and the cartoon gendarmes board our bus. We disembark and stand in a line on the side of the motorway. Our bags in front of us. We are instructed to roll up our sleeves to show we have no track marks on our arms. I feel bad for the crew, Mikey, Big Neil and Adam – they didn't want any part of this. I just hope that those on-the-spot-fine rumours are true. The Marseilles dope is hidden inside the spare wheel, but the cops don't even need to bother looking there. They have found what they wanted. Rockford has cheekily stashed some stash – either all for himself or as a decoy – in a jar of hair gel; the sniffer dog has a fit. The gendarmes are beside themselves with smugness, petting and fussing over the excitable doggy. You would think the mutt had just won Crufts. They march Barney off to some silly hut by the motorway toll and we wait. Half an hour later and he's back, the tour float a few thousand francs lighter. The police are overbearingly friendly. Cracking jokes about our naughtiness and bidding us a safe journey.

This is at least a bit closer to the kind of corruption I can understand. I have incidentally found out that Martin Carr shares a flat with some toadie *NME* journalist (never refer to a journalist as a hack, it is far too flattering). It's just a hunch, but perhaps this is the reason for the Boo Radleys' current high regard in the British music press. We are all going to drown in a tidal wave of sleaze.

Paris in the Terror. The forcible abolition of the Ancien Regime. Louis XVI has been sent to the guillotine. Let the mass executions begin. Tonight is the last night of the tour and the Auteurs are headlining La Cigalle, a beautiful eighteenth-century ballroom in Pigalle. Outside whores get on with the business of the evening. Inside the Boo Radleys are soundchecking, play-fighting and kicking a football around the stage. A Boo Radley miskicks and the ball lands insolently at my feet. By now the kind of welcome I expect. I kick as hard as I can. Give the fucker the alehouse ball. It catches Martin Carr square on the head.

'Ay, can't youse fookin' kick straight or wha'?' whines the Scouse Brian Wilson.

'Oh I can fucking kick straight, pal,' I retort.

The show is masterful. I start off solo and acoustic. I strum the opening bars of 'Housebreaker' while the curtains are still closed. As the drapes go back the audience gasp. It is as if I've been there since the beginning of time (if we'd been on before the Boo Radleys I'd have made sure I was on until the end of time). Oh hell, it's just one of those evenings. I'm so good that the show's gay promoter (complete with false teeth) tries to pull me. Naturally I decline his amorous advances: 'Vous cassez vous peu de poof.' I smile.

'Ha ha. Fuck you, you Engleesh sheet,' he shoots back, flashing me a mouth full of blackening dentures. This is the third or fourth time I have been called an 'Engleesh sheet' in this country; perhaps it's good that we are going home. We head back to the ferry terminal straight after the show. I started out this tour feeling like William Joyce, the Irish-American Nazi propagandist who came to be known as Lord Haw Haw. A traitor in exile. Now drunk, and drunk on success, I feel more like the Duke of Wellington. The salarymen snuggle up conspiratorially in the back of the bus.

'I feel like I've been on tour with Motorhead,' says Rockford. Lightweight.

Late November. 'Lenny Valentino' has a midweek chart position of 35. Its highest actual chart position is 41. Pulp's 'Lipgloss', released the same week, reaches 48. Small victories.

9

Colonel Klutz

December 1993. End-of-year round-ups in the music press. American bands still holding up – all polls feature Nirvana, Lemonheads, Belly and the Juliana Hatfield Three. Tindersticks *by the Tindersticks is album of the year in* Melody Maker. New Wave *is at number 19. In the NME Writers' Top Fifty Albums of the Year Bjork's* Debut *is number one, and* New Wave *comes in at 18. In* Select *magazine* New Wave *is voted the seventh-best album of the year. And the best album of 1993 as voted for by the writers of* Select: Giant Steps *by the Boo Radleys. Suede lurk around the top three of most critics' polls, and Mr Blobby gets the Christmas number one in the singles chart.*

The singer – who could now pass for an East End villain – has me pinned against the wall. After our, ahem, early-evening opening slot there had been an ominous knock on the dressing-room door.

'Can I have a word – outside?' says the singer, gesturing grimly towards me. Drunk and stoned post-gig, I follow obediently. I know what's coming. I orchestrated it so I'm looking forward to it. Quick as a flash the headline act pulls off some nifty pugilistic footwork and squares up to me. *Jesus, what a knucklehead.* I hadn't imagined his reaction to my onstage comments would be quite as physical. True, last night, with righteous anger and adrenalin raging through my veins I had been spoiling for a fight, but now I just wanted to be sacked – minus pasting.

'How much of a fucking prick are you gonna look when I kick the shit out of you onstage?' the singer asks unreasonably. It's a good question, and one that I assume is rhetorical. I drift off into a vision of myself being chased around the stage by a man in a gorilla suit, the gorilla's clumsy paws finally managing to grab me by the scruff of the neck before drop-kicking me high into the air to the whooping delight of the audience. Oh man, that would be entertainment.

'Well, answer me, you fucking cunt.' Not rhetorical then. I snap out of my reverie and slump back against the wall. I'm back in the playground about to take a hiding from a dim bully. There's nothing to do but let the scene play out. Shouldn't take long.

November 1993. Undaunted by my recent travails and in defiant mood, I go back into the studio to begin work on the follow-up to *New Wave*. When I recorded the first album there was only one problem: at times the real band had to become a fake band. If there was a flaw in any of Alice's bass parts then I would quickly repair them – to save money and time. Likewise Glenn's drumming: any errors would be covered up with a bit of overdubbed percussion or a sleight-of-hand edit. Now, with the addition of Rockford and the Cellist – both consummate musicians – the fake band is now in the recording studio, hot to trot, and wanting to be a real band. Phil Vinall is also flailing. He knows that after the first album the record company want to get a 'big' producer on board. Gil Norton? Flood? David Lynch. *Sorry, did you say David*

Lynch? The film director? I decline all these kind offers and stick with Vinall. Trouble is, with the prior knowledge that the record company have tried to usurp him, and after the Mercury fiasco and near miss of 'Lenny Valentino', Phil Vinall is acting like a spooked horse.

After a couple of weeks laborious recording, Vinall and I adjourn to the shitty-brown-walled Roundhouse studios in Chalk Farm to start mixing. In the gloom of the studio the mixes sound good but I'm not sure, so after a week I take the tracks home to listen to. Oh Christ, they sound terrible. 'New French Girlfriend', my cool glib pop song about not much at all, has now metamorphosed into a muddy cock-rocking club-footed ogre – and it's still not about anything.

Stadium-sized guitars bounce off the walls. Everything sounds as though it was recorded through a sock. 'Modern History', once a stately acoustic ballad, is now an overlong plodder, and 'The Upper Classes' – one of my best songs to date – is just ugly. The only tracks that sound any good are a throwaway song called 'Daughter of a Child' and a re-recording of 'Lenny Valentino', but I've had as much of that one as I can take. In the midst of all this we have a touring obligation. So remixing and re-recording – of which there will be plenty – will have to wait until the New Year.

On paper it was unpromising. In real life it looked even worse. The Auteurs are booked to support Matt Johnson's band The The on a UK tour. All of this organised months in advance, before the recent setbacks, when life was a breeze and I would skip over lawns of freshly mown grass without a care in my head, laughing and doffing my hat to a cartoon bluebird as I bent down to pick a buttercup.

Tour with The The? Sure, if it keeps everyone happy and it sells some more records, why not? My levity lasts for about a day and a half.

Reality dawns. The truth is, I don't care too much for Matt Johnson. He's some guy who sold a ton of records in the 80s, and now he's got some new dreck he's trying to flog. Coincidentally, some of the work on the new Auteurs album has been done at a recording studio owned by one Matt Johnson. The studio walls are covered in terrible paintings: some recognisable originals of The The album sleeves, others perhaps specially commissioned. The theme of the paintings seems to be ghastly men and ghastly women giving in to all manner of bodily functions with grim abandon. Oh, and imminent nuclear destruction. A clear indication of Johnson's faultless yet simplistic world view. *Human race: awful. Never mind, will probably be extinguished in some sort of self-inflicted Armageddon. Told you so. The bastards deserved it*. As I said, sold a lot of records in the 80s.

On no account attempt to tour the UK in December. Your limbs will become brittle with cold as you trundle up and down the country in a freezing tour bus and no one will come to your gigs as they are attending Christmas parties. Christmas parties in *your* hotel. Oh yes, the late-night bars of the Holiday Inn, Ibis and Radisson hotels – the après-gig drinking stations of the lower- to mid-level rock band. Every nook and cranny of these corporate flophouses taken over by drunken reps and violent drones from the frightening world of real honest work. Civvy Street – pissed up, embittered, trying to get over another empty year and on your fucking case.

The Comedian. The straw that broke the singer-wearing-the-camel-coat's back. Johnson has got his buddy, some unfunny stand-up,[14] to do a slot on the London date of the tour, at the Brixton Academy, in an attempt to inject some much-needed

[14] Simon Day – Tommy Cockles from tedious 90s catchphrase comedy *The Fast Show*.

mirth into the proceedings. We've already played about ten shows up and down the country, going on at an increasingly early time to fewer and fewer punters. In Liverpool we actually take to the stage as the doors are opening. I'm not used to this shit. Even on the early Suede tours when we'd go on early the venue would still be rammed. I'm cocky and full of it. And I'm also way hipper than Johnson in the press. The Auteurs have not done a support tour for over a year and I know we shouldn't be here. The venues are mostly seated and the audience mainly in their mid-thirties. One night I try and watch some of Johnson's show. It's impossible to tell what the audience make of it, as they sit pinned rigid to their chairs – subjected to another mirthless slow-witted entry from Matt Johnson's diary of doom.

Backstage in Manchester on the first date of the tour we are all seated around the communal trestle dining tables. Summoned by the great man: my band, Johnson's mob, road crews and caterers. Oh God, this is awful. Worse than school. Johnson sits head of the table and bangs his cutlery like a caveman to get our attention. Jesus Christ, he's making some sort of 'Welcome to the Tour' speech. He then orders each member of his American band to introduce themself to us, making them stand up as they do so. The Yanks obey orders, sheepishly giving name, rank and serial number, before sitting back down in shame. I respond in kind, acting like a sullen teenager, mumbling and avoiding eye contact. Johnson's welcome speech is about as inviting as the offer of a refreshing shower at Dachau. It's all designed to say, 'This is my tour. I'm the boss. Step out of line, and I'll kick the shit out of you.' I sink back into my school chair at my school table and think to myself that I want to die. Actually, on second thoughts, I want Matt Johnson to die.

'So the comedian is going on *after* us? We're going on at 7.30

when the doors open, and we're supporting a fucking comedian?' Me to Manager Tony. 'And since when has the fucking comedian been on the bill?'

'Urgh, hum, er . . . since yesterday,' splutters Manager Tony.

We hit the stage running. A blistering 15-minute set. If we have to go on early we may as well get out early. And before anyone can say 'Spinal Tap' and 'Puppet Show' we're off . . . with one parting shot from me.

'Thanks a lot, I hope you enjoy the comedian. In fact he'll be followed by another comedian called Matt Johnson.' A few cheers, a few heckles, nothing much because there's not that many people here. Not the wittiest one-liner in the world, but it doesn't matter, for this is not the real damage that I intend to inflict. I am now apoplectic with rage. I stalk through the corridors of the Brixton Academy hurling abuse. Outside Johnson's dressing room there is a rack of guitars waiting to be taken to the side of the stage. I summon up a lungful of phlegm and flob it over a Strat at the front of the rack. I then take a flying leap at the guitars – luckily they're sturdy and feel hardly any pain from my aerial attack. Next, it's into the heart of darkness to confront Colonel Klutz. I hammer on the dressing-room door calling him a wanker and a cunt and shouting how I'm going to 'fucking kill him'. It's a sorry spectacle, but thankfully it doesn't get any worse. Matt Johnson is not in his dressing room. Why would he be? It's only a quarter to eight.

'Well, answer me, you cunt?' The band have heard the commotion and come out of the dressing room. Alice is first to my defence as usual, but Klutz is having none of it: 'You're as bad as him.'

Alice laughs at Matt Johnson, in that way that only women can. It's the laugh that hurts more than any witty riposte ever will.

Johnson is temporarily floored. Emasculated. Then he regains his footing, and his balls. Turning to Barney: 'And you're a wanker too. You've all been wankers since day one, apart from you,' he says, pointing at the Cellist.

This is great, better than I could have hoped for, as the Cellist in the spirit of camaraderie tries to remonstrate with Matt Johnson by assuring him that he too is a wanker.

For the first time in my life I find myself agreeing with him. But I realise that, fun though this is, it may go on for some time. 'Do you want to throw us off the tour then?' I ask the colonel.

'Do you want me to throw you off the tour?' Klutz asks me back, quizzically and more reasonably than before, brow ever so slightly furrowed.

Finally, the sound of a thousand pennies dropping from a thousand fruit machines, all hitting the jackpot simultaneously crash into Matt Johnson's eardrum then wearily make the long journey to his brain. 'Right. You're sacked,' he barks at us. Then lumbers off back to his cave. Pleased with his work. What a fucking dunce.

10

Russian Futurists black out the sun

January 1994. The first music press front covers of the year are traditionally a bold prediction of who is going to dazzle like no one else has dazzled before, reaping unimaginable rewards for themselves, and for the rest of us change the way we perceive the dimensions of time and space. For their first issue of the year NME *stick Elastica on the front cover. During the first week of the new year Blobby is still number one. Time and space remain unaltered.*

Russia, 1914. Filippo Tommasa Marinetti, poet, polemicist, propagandist and founder of Italian Futurism, expects a hero's welcome when he pays a visit to his Russian counterparts in St Petersburg. The Stray Dog Café, in a dingy cellar, is the hub of the Russian avant-garde. The talk – on the eve of the First World War – is of Futurism. But there is a nasty surprise in store, and the extravagantly moustachioed Marinetti is roundly mocked by the Russian Futurists, who feel they have moved on from the Italian's shallow fetishism of machines and his derivative assimilations of Braque and

Picasso. Marinetti is denounced as an attention-seeker. The Russians have a point.[15]

Harecourt House, Royal College Street, Camden Town, London NW1, 7 January 1994. The cramped two-bedroom flat is in a rundown 60s council block. Phil Vinall is temporarily staying with ex-Suede manager Jon Eydmann. In nine years time and just 200 yards further up the road, necrophiliac Anthony John Hardy will be found guilty of the murder of three prostitutes after human remains are found in bin bags behind a Royal College Street pub. Back in Jon Eydmann's drab front room the necrophilia has begun in earnest. Donna Matthews has plugged her Fender Telecaster into the hi-fi and is playing along with a Wire album – *Manscape*. Of course she's note perfect.

Donna Matthews and Justin Welch from Elastica are also staying in Jon's crowded flat. Vinall produced their first single 'Stutter' and is now sifting through the band's demos trying to squeeze an album out of them. Donna, although she doesn't realise it, is a negative Welsh Timothy Leary figure. Arriving in London from Newport with just an electric guitar and enough heroin for the movers and shakers of the Camden scene to turn on, tune in and nod out. Pure rock 'n' roll. 'Can you buy me a drink and lend me a tenner? We're doing a photo shoot for Italian *Vogue* tomorrow.'

Donna and drummer boy Justin are the stars in their own

[15] Marinetti also received short shrift from the great Vorticist Wyndham Lewis. In the first issue of *Blast* Lewis writes, 'Automobilism (Marinetteism) bores us. We do not want to go about making a hullabaloo about motor cars, any more than about knives and forks, elephants or gas pipes.' Lewis also asserted that Britain had founded Futurism some 150 years ago. It was called the Industrial Revolution.

modern-day Shelagh Delaney morality play. Wide-eyed country kids who accidentally corrupt the cynical city dwellers while being corrupted by the big city itself. Despite all this I like these two a lot.

Jon Eydmann has a vague notion that the Auteurs and Elastica should release a split single on his new record label. The plan is that we will each cover one of the other's songs. Donna claims she wants to record a version of 'Junk Shop Clothes', although for my part well I don't want to record any Elastica tunes, but I haven't quite been able to broach this small inconvenience with Jon or Donna. It won't be a problem though, for there is a far greater obstacle for them to surmount than my sniffiness about Elastica's songwriting capabilities: Justine Frischmann.

Frischmann is a drag, an ambitious media arriviste – even less rock 'n' roll than the Cellist – but with a couple of impeccable notches on her bedpost: Brett Anderson and now Damon Albarn. I haven't paid much attention to Albarn until recently, but now the fucker seems to be popping up all over the press, always with something bitchy to say about my band or Suede. The man is becoming a pest. Clearly he *has* been paying attention. The first time I see Damon and Justine together they are practically dragging each other along Camden High Street. A gruesome couple. A pair of greedy hobgoblins, knocking down small children in their path, batting away passers-by and anyone they perceive as a possible threat to their rise to the top.

Blur have recently been on the slide but their second album *Modern Life Is Rubbish* sadly seems to have saved their bacon. The damn thing was released over six months ago, yet they're still managing to cream off hit singles from the fucker. Outwardly and publicly I slag the record off, but secretly I have a soft spot for it. 'For Tomorrow' is even a retarded classic with cynical, clumsy references to the Westway. Boy, this band give the public what they want. Of course I *would* like their album: they've copped the best bits from Suede and the Auteurs and then dressed them up in a mod suit. In parts this album sounds like a Secret Affair tribute act taking on the Members to see who can come last in a battle-of-the-bands competition. Blur, no fucking problem. Oh Christ, I worry to myself. There's going to be another mod revival and I'm going to get blamed for it. This of course does not happen.

So Justine gets wind of the planned Auteurs/Elastica split single and stomps all over it in her big boy boots. I am evidently persona non grata. It would seem that the head girl is not too keen on the talented ones in her group hanging out with yours truly. Good God, she thinks I'm problematic; does the poor girl not understand the insidiousness within her own ranks? It's like a version of Joseph Losey's *The Servant* with Donna in the Dirk Bogarde role, the malevolent butler, to Justine's upper-class dimwit played by James Fox. In the film the butler takes over the house and then dismantles every aspect of his master's psyche. In reality the drugs rip through Elastica like Hurricane Satan.[16]

So, as I have leapt forward in time I will allow my twenty-first-century self to explain my 'position' on Britpop. *Modern Life Is Rubbish* by Blur is often cited as the first Britpop album. Not so. Suede were without doubt the first Britpop band. Their first single 'The Drowners' was released in May '92. The Auteurs' first album

[16] Years later Donna Matthews' new band Klang – a cool Fall/Ut hybrid – are invited to support Black Box Recorder on a jaunt around the country. A good chance to catch up and talk about the old days? It's all gone. Donna has no memory of the author or indeed the old days. Britpop: if you were there, then you probably cannot remember it.

was released some months before *Modern Life* . . . and a few weeks before Suede's debut. So technically *New Wave* pips it. Only problem is that lyrically – with the theme being more Gloria Swanson in *Sunset Boulevard* than Walthamstow Dog Stadium – the album does not fit, even within Britpop's nebulous remit. Even as recently as 2007 Simon Reynolds mistakenly concluded in an essay for his book *Bring the Noise* that the Auteurs song 'American Guitars' is an 'anti-grunge anthem'. *Suede*, musically rooted in English rock 1972–4, does fit the bill. If you possess the wrong kind of ambition it can be easy to fall between the cracks. There is also a case for Denim's retro seminal *Back in Denim* being a Britpop prototype, but y'know *it's Lawrence* . . . Back to the twentieth century. Early part.

In 1913, the same year that Stravinsky's *Rite Of Spring* caught Paris unawares, leaving the audience reeling with contempt and self-righteous indignation, Russian Futurists from St Petersburg staged an opera about a group of astronauts who wage war on the sun, killing and burying it. Now that the sun is dead, a new reality can be defined. The opera is called *Victory over the Sun*.

And now I am about to be usurped. With *New Wave* – my own *Victory over the Sun*, my own new reality. Like Matiushin and Kruchenykh, the bold authors of *Victory over the Sun*, with their war against vulgar Marinetti, I am about to be thrown into a war that I cannot win – with the burgeoning Britpoppers, all brightly coloured and bold as brass. If you possess the wrong kind of ambition, you fall between the cracks.

11

Commercial failure

February–March 1994. Number-one albums by Chaka Demus and Pliers, Tease Me, *and Tori Amos,* Under the Pink. *'Things Can Only Get Better' by D:ream is number one in the UK singles chart.*

The commercial failure of 'Lenny Valentino' back in November hadn't bothered me that much: a few chairs thrown across the room, the odd door shaken about on its hinges. Of the newish British guitar bands only Suede and the Manic Street Preachers are selling more records than us. Blur, I conclude, don't count as they won't be in it for the long haul. Pulp's single 'Lipgloss' received even more airplay and press coverage than 'Lenny V' and charted seven places lower than yours truly. Oddly, no one in the Pulp camp claims to be that concerned about just missing out on the top 40.

'Top 75!' exclaims drummer Nick Banks. 'After all these years we could hardly believe we made the charts,' he adds guilefully. *Oh yeah*, I think to myself. *Well you didn't make the charts, pal, same as me*. Nonetheless, there is a marked difference in attitude from my own manager, producer and record company, who are moping around as if someone or something has just died.

March 1994: The commercial failure of 'Chinese Bakery' doesn't bother me that much. Another of those fairly regular trips to A & E with badly swollen knuckles after trying to punch my way through a door, some broken crockery. Nothing major. 'Chinese Bakery' peaks at number 42. Oh good, one place lower than the last single. And about seven places lower than the recent Pulp single 'Do You Remember the First Time?'[17] – their first to crack the top 40. Bastards. 'Chinese Bakery'. What the fuck was I thinking about? It's a better song than it is a record. In the same way that 'Lenny Valentino' is a better record than it is a song. Don't confuse this argument with semantics. Just think for reference 'Good Vibrations' – fantastic record, terrible song.[18] So 'Chinese Bakery' is about last year's trip to New York. Brenda Khan's in there and the Toulouse-Lautrec reference is little Marty Diamond.

Rich Bohemians slumming it with the poor. Same subject matter as Pulp's soon-to-be-written 'Common People' but set in the wrong fucking country and about the wrong fucking singer. Just as I am about to release an album with such an un-English title as 'Now I'm a Cowboy', every other fucker seems to be dusting

[17] It takes a huge effort for Pulp to get into the charts. With a launch party at the ICA accompanied by a short film, also called *Do You Remember the First Time?* in which Jarv asks some interesting people (Viv Stanshall) and some uninteresting people (Justine Frischmann) about losing their cherry. My twenty-first-century self would have to concede that in 1994 Pulp were a little more on the zeitgeist than the Auteurs.

[18] Also see the entire career of Marc Bolan: rotten songs, fabulous records.

off their mam's and dad's old Tommy Steele records. With two singles stalling outside the top 40 and the new album due for release in a couple of weeks, expectations have been lowered somewhat.

When I listen to the original mixes for the album, it's clear I've gone and served up a fucking dog's dinner. Unbeknown to me, Phil Vinall has become obsessed with some rickety Keith Richards solo album and has decided that my record should be given the organic Keith treatment. The mixes are woody, dry and stillborn. I give Vinall a dressing-down and we block-book the studio for endless remixing and re-recording, hiring in every state-of-the-art piece of recording equipment in the process.

At the beginning of the year Alice and I move into a two-up-two-down Georgian townhouse in the heart of Camden Town. I hate the house immediately – my old manor of Southgate was like the fucking Cotswolds compared to this. By February '94 Camden High Street seems to be cluttered up with little mods, all carrying guitars and heading towards the very same rehearsal studios where the Auteurs practise their cruel art. Every morning I rise early, leave my hated new house, march the few hundred yards up Camden Road to Royal College Street, lean on the door buzzer, wake up the junkies, kick Phil Vinall out of bed and drag him into the studio to make him fix the mess that he and I have created. All other band members are told politely but firmly to stay at home.

A large part of the problem – leaving aside the Keith solo album issue – is that there has been so much dope smoking at the recording sessions, mainly by me, that the album sounds like it is at war with itself. Struggling to break out of its classic Kinks songwriting foundations and taking a walk down Main Street Kingston JA, stopping only to hang out with Dr Alimantado (just to let him know his fly is undone) before giving it the pimp roll to meet Rockers at King Tubby's – gotta lay down some dub plates. Is there ever a good time to discover reggae? Oh God. The only thing to do with this turd is to polish it.

The studio, by the time we've filled it with all the hired gear that our vast budget can afford, looks like an epileptic's worst nightmare. It's impossible not to meet the eye of some horny mechanical aural exciter trying it on with a bit of winking and blinking. 'I'm a Rich Man's Toy' is the first song we work on. It's one of the last things recorded for the album just before Christmas and straight after the disastrous The The tour. Unsurprisingly the track is fucking furious. It was originally written for Kylie Minogue. My people send her a demo. Her people politely decline.

It's not really Kylie, is it? Kylie goes on to make her 'indie' album a year later with the involvement of various Manic Street Preachers. Of course the album's rubbish. Poor Kylie. We work quickly on 'I'm a Rich Man's Toy'. I add a sleazy vibraphone which I cannot play, and we buff and shine. Result: the sound of sheet metal crashing through an iceberg then plunging deep into an ocean of razor blades. Yep, that's the sound I've been looking for. We apply the same make-up to the re-recording of 'Lenny Valentino', 'Modern History' and 'New French Girlfriend'. 'Underground Movies', one of the album's best tracks, is rescued by ditching everything previously recorded, sending it all into reverse echo and adding more spooky vibraphone. At least 'The Upper Classes' is finally saved from the abyss, but is still nowhere near as good as the BBC session version recorded a few months later. For weeks and weeks we scratch and polish until neither Phil nor I can take any more. I'm pretty sure we've done, at the very least, a great salvage job on the album, but I know in my heart that this is not good enough. I suspect I have a bloated corpse on my hands, and on my conscience.

Album playback time – Dave Boyd from Hut Recording and Keith Wood from the American label, Vernon Yard, are coming down to the studio to hear the new mixes. We're done for; this is the same Dave Boyd who hated 'Lenny Valentino' when it was a single. Now he's gonna have another ten tracks that he can hate along with it. Boy, it's gonna be a fun evening.

Vinall turns the lights down low in time-honoured studio playback tradition. Boyd, looking more and more like Greg Allman as the months pass, skins up.

'Let's listen on the Ronnies,' says Phil ominously, as he cranks the master volume to three quarters and switches over from the regular studio speakers to the huge speakers built into the wall.[19] Within seconds a terrifying noise threatens to sever the top of my head. I try to catch a look at the two A & R men. Do they like it? I can't actually see as I am pinned to my chair by sheer volume. Phil knows we're in the shit so he's overcompensating with sonic terrorism. Fuck, his ploy is even working on me. This album is starting to sound pretty good. Phil cranks the volume that last quarter up to full. Oh Jesus, I'm experiencing maximum g. I succeed in turning my head slightly. Out of the corner of my eye I can see their little legs tapping, and yes, here it comes, the heads nodding along, sagely and out of time. The A & R boys love it. What a pair of complete and utter bozos.

[19] Recording studio terminology. Usually in a studio environment recorded sound is monitored on regular-sized speakers i.e. Yamaha NS 10s. Sometimes, when a mix has just been completed the producer/engineer wants to listen to his endeavours at eardrum-perforating volume on the largest speakers available in the studio. Big speakers = biggies = Ronnie Biggs = Ronnies.

Keith Wood, head of Hut's brand new US division, is buying the drinks after the album playback. He and Boyd are blown away. The album sounds fantastic; it's got exactly the right sound for the American market, apparently. The market that we are going to be 'cracking'. 'Lenny Valentino' is going to be the first US single from the new album, and Keith reckons it will be all over the radio stateside. As the A & R guys burble on to each other, talking shop, I gaze off into the middle distance, imagining a nation of Chocolate Teapots nervously fiddling with their radio dials, panicking at the loss of their beloved Cheap Trick, unable to escape me as they switch from one classic rock station to another.

When the first album came out I was sometimes flattered by the ecstatic reviews, but never surprised and never relieved. The album deserved nothing less. Now, to my huge surprise and immense relief, the reviews for *Now I'm a Cowboy* are unanimously fucking great. Nothing below four stars across the board. It's a weird time. You know you've delivered something substandard and yet everyone still loves it – this situation will be reversed several times over the coming years.

With another bit of twenty-first-century hindsight applied I should state that – out of context – I now view *Now I'm a Cowboy* as a fucking classic. Sure it was rushed initially, and there are production issues (less so than any other record of the mid-90s period), but it does stand up better than most of its contemporaries. It's just that it was possibly the worst kind of record to release in 1994. Fuck, I didn't see that one coming: the public aren't going to put up with another mod revival are they? Surely not. Oh God, here comes Phil Daniels. Not content with the full horror of his acting he's going to torture me with his appearance on Blur records. In years to come they will refer to this kind of collusion as an Axis of Evil. Bandy leg dancing. Dick Van Dyke *dahn at the dogs. Parklife! Parklife!* It'll all be over by Christmas. Please God, make it stop. It has to get worse before it can get better. Can it actually get worse? I think to myself. Oh yes.

The commercial failure of *Now I'm a Cowboy* when it is eventually released in May doesn't bother me that much, just a few broken . . . Oh you get the picture. Thing is, it's not really a failure: the album peaks at number 17 in the British charts and even hangs around for a few weeks. It goes top ten in a couple of Scandinavian countries. Jesus, this is pretty good going; none of my favourite groups ever made the charts. The fact that I'm in the fucking top 20 is a surprise and a relief. After the last two singles I was fearing the worst. (Don't worry, that comes soon enough.) Apparently though, my own successes and failures are all part of some intrinsically linked cosmology, which has nothing to do with art and goes by the name of context. Blur release their annoying *Parklife* album at approximately the same time as *Now I'm a Cowboy*. It sells 46 billion copies in Swindon alone and the world changes forever. From this point onward anything that sells less than 46 billion is deemed a resounding failure. We are now on a different trajectory.

12

It's a great time to be dead

March–early June 1994. 'Girls and Boys' by Blur goes top five. Oasis' first single 'Supersonic' makes the top 40. It is all kicking off. On 7 April, two days after you know who, ace Brit R & B howler Lee Brilleaux dies of lymphoma. Nirvana's new single 'Penny Royaltea' is pulled from the release schedule. The B-side is called 'I Hate Myself And I want to Die'. The Auteurs' second album Now I'm a Cowboy, *released 9 May, goes top 20 in the UK album charts. Weekly music press have got a hard-on for S*M*A*S*H. At the end of May Man United FC top the singles chart with 'Come on You Reds'.*

'You've been offered a short support tour of Scandinavia with Nirvana,' says Manager Tony on the other end of the line. Everett True, a journalist and friend of Kurt Cobain, has given the Nirvana singer a copy of my first album. Of course I want to do the tour.

A few days later the phone rings. Tony again, unusual for a Saturday night. There's a rumour going around that Kurt has committed suicide in Rome. This turns out to be untrue. What really happens is that on 4 March Kurt Cobain overdoses on 50

Rohypnol prescription painkiller tablets washed down with champagne in a hotel suite in Rome. He wakes in hospital after spending five days in a coma. Incidentally, our support tour is still said to be going ahead. This is rather optimistic.

This time there is no need for a phone call. News breaks on the radio that Kurt Cobain has died in his Seattle mansion. Probably on 5 April. The body is found two days later by a workman, Gary Smith, hired to install security lights. Kurt died of a gunshot wound to the head. The verdict is suicide.

It could never have happened without Kurt Cobain, alive *or* dead. But it was the singer's death that signalled a sea change in the British music scene. This Britpop thingy that has been bubbling away can finally stand on its own two feet, now that the colossus of Kurt has been vanquished. If, and it's a very big if, after *Nevermind* Cobain had embraced his superstardom and rejected the artistic dead end of *In Utero* and, like, decided to carry on living, then I seriously doubt whether the mindless northern bluff of the Gallagher brothers would have got a look-in.[20] Of course Blur's irritating *Parklife* was already doing brisk business, and Pulp's *His 'n' Hers* had sold well, but without the abrupt but hardly unexpected end of Nirvana, there would have been no light-entertainment battle for number one between Blur and Oasis. No Young British Artists. No Cool Britannia. Nirvana were too much of a force of nature. Not only did Kurt Cobain rudely kill himself, he went and left the bloody door open on his way out. But before Britpop can announce its arrival fully formed, the UK music press is cowardly

[20] OK, it is far-fetched but consider this: initial reviews for the Gallaghers' watery psychedelia were unimpressive before Cobain's death. This in the mid-90s when the early reaction from the music press to a new band was crucial.

insisting that we have one more dry run. The 'New Wave of New Wave' arrives unheralded and unwanted, and hangs around for about a month. Groups of men who are old enough to know better pretend to be gangs of speeding punks in areas of urban decay, and pose for photos beneath silly graffiti slogans. Now close your eyes and count to three. When you open your eyes the memory will be gone, and I will never mention the New Wave of New Wave again.

The Auteurs have gained a new member: Steve 'Chalker' Walker. Chalker, like Elastica's drummer Justin Welch, is a veteran of early-90s garage rockers Spitfire. Chalker is a good old-fashioned choppy rhythm guitarist who doesn't know how to play that many chords – this is actually more promising that it sounds. I like the unreconstructed Steve Walker, despite his ridiculous mockneyisms and his skittlish walk and his useless retro-mod Adidas stylings. Of course he's not that bothered about being in the Auteurs; he'd probably rather be in Elastica like his old band mate Justin, or at the very least with any one of the new breed of weedy Britpoppers. None of this matters. What I really like about Chalker is how much the Cellist pompously loathes him. At this point I have become a fully fledged cunt.

I'm doing the mind guerrilla. May '94 and we set off around the country. We were three, then four, and now we are five. How the hell did I let that happen? I see this tour – the biggest venues we've played so far – as more of an opportunity to play mind games rather than actually promote the new album with my unwanted and ever-growing band. Perhaps we'll be up to six or seven by the end of the tour. That would be nice.

The Auteurs have become a rock band, and like all professional rock bands it is our duty to expand, to become a many-headed

Hydra. A many-headed Hydra with a rock album to promote. We must cut off the Hydra's heads. The problem is I never wanted to be in a rock band. I only like bands at their point of inception. On our tour bus I play back a series of images in my head: old episodes of the Monkees, all living in a house together hungrily waiting for fame, with only their zany adventures to distract them and a ventriloquist's dummy manager for company. A photo of Robert Forster and Grant McLennan taken at the time of the Go Betweens' first single, standing in front of a hand-painted poster bearing the legend 'The Pied Piper Follows Us', Forster preening beneath a bowl haircut, beckoning coquettishly with one silk-gloved hand. A snapshot of Jonathan Richman taken in 1971, looking uptight outside a children's restaurant in his 'favourite jacket'. A picture of Iggy standing in the Asheton brothers' back garden in Ann Arbor. David Essex in *That'll Be the Day*, throwing his school books in the stream and bunking his exams to go and work the fairgrounds of austere early-50s rock 'n' roll Britain with Ringo Starr – Starr back to his best Rory Storm and the Hurricanes look. The fantasy, that's what it's all about. The fantasy of being in a great rock 'n' roll band as opposed to being in a professional rock band. Whatever fame you get, that moment on the cusp of success is always the best. I eject the tape and listen to Chalker going on about birds with big knockers, and booze, and all his mates in bands, and how he loves the 'biz'. If I squint my eyes and only half listen, I could pretend I'm in a scene from *Stardust*. Then he ruins it.

''Ere, boss, do you mind if I put me *Squeeze Greatest Hits* tape on?'

Yes. I do.

However much I am against my own band, I have to concede that although there is an unwanted Faces element creeping in, the five-piece Auteurs are sounding quite marvellous. On a day off from the tour we record a Radio 1 session, this time finally nailing 'The Upper Classes' and turning a throwaway B-side, 'Everything You Say Will Destroy You', into a monster. When the songs are aired on the wireless, some weeks later, the Radio 1 evening session presenters are palpably awestruck as 'The Upper Classes' comes to a halt after seven prowling minutes. *You may as well stop broadcasting right now*, I think to myself, because it doesn't get any better than that. We put in an appearance on *Later with Jools Holland*. It's just a muso fest, not much cop. At least we get to jam with Aswad.

'You have a lady bass player,' booms an Aswad, the ganja not affecting his powers of perception one jot.

And so our tour trundles on. My alcohol and chemical intake has increased to quite prodigious levels, Alice being the only one remotely concerned. The rest of the band would quite happily see me dead. The trouble is I am paying their wages. Alice is also the reason I have to put an end to the Chalker-related tensions that I am enjoying so much.

The 'band' call a 'band meeting'. *Ahahaha*. Rockford and the Cellist petition me to fire Chalker. I don't know if they have any ultimatums planned, I don't allow the situation to progress. To their surprise I immediately concur with them. I can tell from the Cellist's face that he thinks he has scored a major victory over me. *It's not for you, sunshine. Do you think I care about your opinions?* I let them savour their win for a few minutes and then tell them that I have one condition. I will sack Chalker, but only after the next American tour. What can they do but agree? Come the time and I do the deed, Steve Walker takes it well. Somehow, shortly after this the Cellist lets slip to someone, who then lets slip to someone else at the *NME*, that the Auteurs fired their rhythm guitarist for being too working class. *Faaantastic*. I don't even bother denying it. I've gained a reputation for being a bastard, and now I actually am one anyway. Besides, with all these lightweight oiky new bands on the rise, it doesn't do the Auteurs any harm to increase their haughty reputation. Of course I get my way, and Chalker doesn't actually get sacked; he just gets told he's been sacked a lot. He's a good sport, I guess. Steve survives another three Auteurs tours until I dismiss him good and proper, just before we start rehearsing for *After Murder Park*. It's probably safe to say that he's not too shocked and saw it coming.

By June '94 I'm seriously wondering whether I've had enough. Tony and the record company keep bleating about exciting things happening in America. I want it all to end but for some reason I just can't stop. I feel compelled to see this thing through. Also, the oiks are gaining momentum. Crap new comedy band Oasis are wowing 'em in the aisles, and they swarm over them like flies on shit. Maybe it's a good time to get away to America. Kurt Cobain has only been *gone* a few months – and now this. He's lucky. It really is a great time to be dead.

13

Loads of drugs

June 1994. Oasis, initially derided by the music press are quickly re-evaluated and lauded. Pulp's His 'n' Hers *marketed as a debut album, goes to number nine in the UK album charts. Echobelly scrape into the top forty singles chart.*

I'm standing in the designated smoking area of the Airbus, drawing hard on a cigarette, getting in the way of the cabin crew, thinking about what that pilot had told me in the bar: *3600 degrees, the temperature of a jet engine, hot enough to turn iron or steel into liquid.* Irrational fear of flying, that's what they call it. Irrational? What is irrational about not wanting to be propelled through the air in soft metal? I've lost count of the number of flights I've taken since the beginning of the year. The way I see it is that every take-off slashes my odds – increasing my chances of horrific death in mid-air obliteration. I am not scared of dying per se, it's just that when the plane is ascending I can't help imagining the moment of impact and the ensuing ball of flames that will engulf my body. Or maybe, I think as the plane bumps and lurches toward cruising altitude, I will be catapulted out of the fuselage still strapped to my seat, plummeting through the clouds into a freezing ocean, where I will pass out from shock and drown. I may even end up impaled on a tree just a few feet from terra firma. I will concede that I don't have the healthiest outlook on air travel.

The aircraft has been chartered by the festival promoters. On board as well as the Auteurs are derivative northern boors Oasis, useless prog rockers *The* Verve[21] (our label mates) and one unmentionable but fleetingly successful rock band. The great British Public, in its infinite wisdom, will soon take Oasis and *The* Verve to their hearts. For now we're all in it together, in our happy(ish) pub in the sky, en route to ESSF Airport in Sweden, where we are due to play the Hultsfred festival.

I teeter back to my seat. The 'emergency' vodkas I have been power-necking are having the desired effect, and I am lulled into a false sense of security. Then it happens. Odin has taken a look at his diary and noticed that my number is up. The plane emits a diabolical crunching sound, the shudder of death, then the pilot pulls the aircraft's nose sharply upward. We are embarking on a terrifying sheer assent. At speed. We are clearly taking action to avoid hitting something: a fucking mountain. We miss our unintentional target – the fucking mountain – and begin our descent. Descent perhaps being too gentle a description, implying a graceful flutter to a lesser piste. What actually happens is we dive-bomb at full throttle towards the ocean, trolleys sliding, dollies screaming and oxygen masks dangling. I grip the arm of my chair, losing body

[21] Originally called Verve. This group would only start selling records after adding the definite aricle to their name – after a legal tussle with US jazz label Verve – thus becoming *The* Verve. Utterly hopeless. Mass appeal and stupidity are, sadly, intrinsically linked. See also Oasis, U2.

fluid and as ever preparing to die. A tap on my shoulder from the seat behind. Oh for fuck's sake. It's Pete Wolf.

The finger is decorated with self-administered dots inked into the skin. In fact most of Pete's body is covered in tattoos. Not the pretty faux-Oriental designs popular with modern sportsmen or boy bands. Oh no, these are the tattoos of the prison yard, the merchant seaman, the inner-city firm. Pete 'Wolfie' Wolf. Uber roadie. In the past he's worked for us, but today he's working for *The* Verve and Oasis. If we were back in school again – which on this little sortie we are – then Pete Wolf is the school bully. When it's home time you'd better run like hell. Signet rings and biker bracelets clink away like the locks on borstal doors, as Pete Wolf drums his bully beat on the back of my headrest. A bell rings in my head – oh fuck, it's playtime.

'All wight?' he spits into my ear.

'Not really,' I weakly respond

'Fack off, this is real flying,' he consoles. 'Listen, my boys are gonna fackin' 'ave it with that lot of cunts,' he says, gesturing towards the unmentionable rock group. 'When we get to the airport it's gonna fackin' kick off big time.' Pirate Pete then leans back in his seat and sniffs very loudly, just to leave us in no doubt as to what he has been up to. I turn to Mikey our sound engineer, hoping for sentience as we hurtle toward the inevitable.

'Don't worry,' says Mikey. 'If we crash at least we take this lot with us.' I manage a smile. Now I am ready to die.

'This is a call for Mike Hunt. Would Mike Hunt go to the information desk,' announces a Swedish accent over the tannoy. We've been in the country five minutes and Pete Wolf's already started. He's cleared customs and he's pleased with his work, grinning like a moron over in arrivals. I'm elated to be alive, and not even the prospect of 48 hours of Pete Wolf's low-level wit can ruin my mood. I show my passport and a customs officer gestures for me to bring over my hand luggage to be searched.

The customs officer leaves me alone in the holding cell, locking the door behind him. One plastic chair in a bare white room. Eight foot by ten, a high ceiling with a row of small frosted-glass windows at the top of one of the walls. My joie de vivre has been brought crashing to the ground, my elation trampled into the dirt.

'This is not good,' says the customs officer, as he pulls out the first of a seemingly never-ending number of small plastic bags from my hand luggage, variously containing pathetic lumps of hash, forlorn shavings of weed, a couple of crumbly Mogadons and a folded piece of paper with a tiny white powdery stain.

'Not good,' reiterates the officer as if I have personally let him down.

'I know,' I mutter back, feeling chastened and trying hard to sound it.

Finally, the customs officers finish searching my hand luggage. They have accumulated a collection of half a dozen incriminating plastic bags. Onto my jacket and trouser pockets. *Surely not*. I pray to myself. Then the unthinkable: before my own eyes I turn into a drug mule moron magician – it's *Midnight Express* starring Tommy Cooper. From the outside pockets of my leather jacket more and more small plastic sachets start appearing, all containing minuscule amounts of illegal drugs. The customs officers look at each other and then at me, incredulous at my apparently brazen efforts at drug smuggling. They have accumulated quite a large collection of not very dangerous narcotics.

Of course I am no drug mule, but I am a moron. Prior to this Scandinavian festival jaunt I had been to America on a promotional push for the release of the second album. My attitude towards the illegality of certain substances has become pretty relaxed, and I am quite happy to stroll through customs on internal flights in the US with pretty much anything on my personage. It happens. I mean if the record label is prepared to put me up in a bungalow at the Chateau Marmont in Hollywood I'm gonna have some fun, right? So, on the eve of the flight to Sweden – preoccupied with imminent plane crash death as usual – I throw a few essentials into a holdall and shove my passport into the inside pocket of my leather jacket. The same leather jacket and holdall that contain the detritus of the previous week's mild American drug abuse.

It's perhaps the least intrusive strip search that anyone has ever undergone. The searching officer correctly ascertains that there would be no reason for me to hide anything internally when I have practically walked through customs and plonked my eccentric stash down on the counter. The search is wearily completed after a gentle forage, and a quick spread 'em and look up the Khyber. My jailer looks pityingly at me, shakes his head and once again locks me up, making his position quite clear – he thinks I'm a nitwit.

After a long wait I am led out of the cell to be interviewed. A kindly female officer produces a set of scales to weigh up the haul. The officer tries to reassure me that I probably haven't carried in enough illegal contraband to be charged with dealing – a mandatory custodial sentence in Sweden – but she has to weigh it up anyway. It's just under. The officials are at a loss as to what to do with me. The conversation turns to rock festivals, and everyone's mood brightens. *Now I'm a Cowboy* has recently been a top-ten album here and the customs officers are starting to see a way out.

'How many people will you be playing to at the festival?' enquires a benevolent customs man. Force of habit ensures that I start to correct him.

'You mean "playing at".' He doesn't get it. Not the best time for wisecracks, so I answer the question.

'Five thousand, maybe more.' A quick call to the panicky promoters confirms this. So for the good of the Swedish economy and for the good of Anglo-Scandinavian relations I am released. Free to unleash my bad vibes upon an otherwise happy festival crowd.

'You will have to pay a fine of £1500,' says an officer, 'and an extra £500 for your funny joke.'

'Do you take credit cards?' I ask, uncertain as to whether this sounds like another bad joke.

'Cash only,' comes the certain reply.

All drugs are good. All drugs are bad. *I'm no good at taking drugs*. This is absurd: one cannot be good or bad at taking drugs – though conversely there have been times when I have been good at taking a lot of drugs. I just never had the dedication to make it into a full-time career. During the early 80s in provincial England, drugs just did not have the availability they do now. So as a teen my staples were household products, hash and, on a red-letter day, speed. Hash always carried with it a certain amount of shame and, with the year zero clarion call of punk still reverberating through the suburbs, anything that felt even slightly hippyish was considered very bad. Rightly so. Though for some reason hallucinogens were an exception to the rule. So speed it was to be. If it was the preferred narcotic of Lou Reed and Mark Smith then it was good enough for me. However, my asthma and one too many panic attacks stopped me from becoming the youthful speed freak of my dreams. Alcohol became my drug of choice. I'm a good drunk – one of the best you'll ever be lucky enough to meet. Uncle Lou also knew about the booze when he wrote 'The

Power of Positive Drinking'. Booze is my muse. During the mid-90s the Britpop horde devoured the class As like hungry peasants at the eat-as-much-as-you-can meal deal. Really, some of the most unlikely sorts got Dequinceyed up to the gills. Proof, if ever it were needed, that heroin does not always unleash the dark creative beast.

I scuttle back onto the shuttle bus we are sharing with *The* Verve to a slow handclap. Not only have I delayed everyone by two hours – meaning *The* Verve will miss the late-afternoon gig by new best friends Oasis – I have also depleted *The* Verve's tour float. Since the first American tour – when I relieved the Chocolate Teapot of the tour float in the first week, got my pockets rifled and then dispensed with the remainder as though I were Jimmy Stewart in a particularly generous mood – we now travel with as little spare cash as possible. The outcome of this is that *The* Verve have had to bail me out in my moment of need. I certainly wouldn't have done the same for them if the situation had been reversed. Now it's fair to say that *The* Verve have got a bit of a cob on.

'Please don't start any trouble,' says Alice as I slouch down next to her.

I follow her instructions, and even show some gratitude to *The* Verve by allowing them to play their awful 'classic' rock tapes all the way to the festival. *Gimme Shelter, Smile, Skip Spence*, more *Smile, Pet Sounds*, on and on it goes. For two and a half hours we have to suffer the frightful good taste of Richard Ashcroft's record collection. And you know what? I don't say a word.

We just about make our stage time, and the set flies by without much ado. I even thank *The* Verve from the stage 'for their help' – naturally. With a bit of goading from Pete Wolf, this is interpreted by the band, who are watching us from the side of the stage, as some sort of slight against them. 'What the fook is he saying about us?'

I stumble into the hotel room at around three in the morning, Alice is sleeping soundly in the bed. The Jägermeister is taking its toll and I'm just about ready to pass out when it starts.

'You'll never take the north
You'll never take the north
You'll never take the north'

Various members of Oasis and *The* Verve are drunkenly swaggering around in the fountain some 200 yards from my hotel window. At the vanguard, Pete Wolf, obviously. What is taking place is technically known as ''aving it' or alternatively 'kicking off'. A few more verses extolling the greatness of the north of England over the rest of the world and then bewilderingly into a chant of: 'Two World Wars and one World Cup'.

I snap, and simultaneously all the pieces fall into place.

Like many bored visitors to the USA I have become something of a pyromaniac. Many free hours have been filled on the last couple of American tours by visiting local gun and firework shops, idly chatting to their amusing redneck owners and making ludicrous braggadocio purchases. I stumble over to my holdall and root around in the inside zip-up pouch – where the customs officers had neglected to search, probably because they were happy enough with their catch of the day – and pull out the small tool kit that I had carefully smuggled back all the way from JFK and had promptly forgotten about as soon as I got home. I fiddle around with the catches on the box, being careful not to wake sleeping Alice, and prise out the pearl from the oyster: a marvellous loaded vintage German flare gun. How appropriate.

'Fucking cants, fucking cants, fucking cants,' sings a now abandoned Wolfie, teetering on a statue in the fountain, to the tune of '*Here We Go*'. I remember the salesman in the gun shop telling me that this particular flare had an 'awesome three-way report'. I open the balcony doors and crouch down, holding the gun as steady as I can and aim for Pete Wolf's stupid bonce.

Jesus Christ, that salesman wasn't lying: the gun *has* got a fucking awesome three-way report. My God, it looks like the last days of Saigon out there – I'm half expecting to hear Jimi's 'Star Spangled Banner'. Of course I don't hit the errant roadie – my aim is poor – he just thinks he is under mortar attack and dives into the fountain for cover. The flare is so bright he won't have a clue which direction it was fired from. Obviously, I'm sad I didn't hit my target and kill the cunt, but decide to turn in for the night anyway, and before the rescue services arrive. I creep into bed.

Alice stirs. 'Don't you think you've been in enough trouble for one day,' she murmers.

I fall into oblivion, satisfied, temporarily at least.

The hotel staff want us all out. They don't say anything; they just disdainfully serve us black coffee from the breakfast bar, gratis. If we were to pay for our drinks it would prolong our stay, leaving them exposed to our awful Brits-abroad behaviour for more unbearable, life-sapping minutes.

Hungover like hell, dressed from head to toe in morticians' mourning clothes, with a huge black dog clawing my shoulders, I'm in full receipt of the bill. I just hope and pray that I'm not going to be stung for a bloody great tip.

Does he know? Does he know? Pete Wolf is walking towards me with menace. *Does he know?* Menace. Getting closer, with menace. Hold on, he always walks with menace.

'Some *cant* tried to fackin' shoot me last night.'

'Jesus,' I say, feigning surprise.

'Not him, you *cant*,' says Pete, pleased with his rare wit. 'One of that lot over there.' He gestures towards the unmentionable yet fleetingly successful rock band. I think I know what's coming. 'When we get to the airport it's gonna fackin' kick off. Big time.'

We are on the shuttle bus back to ESSF airport. Our travelling companions are the unmentionable rock band, who are now, somewhat late in the day, getting in on the rowdy act. I can't stand this hooligan braying between bands, though I have to concede that my anonymous contribution to proceedings has hardly had a calming influence. *Whatever happened to the witty riposte?* I wonder to myself as a beer can sails by my head.

'Is Mike Hunt on board the aircraft? Would Mike Hunt please make himself known to one of the cabin crew.' Alice and I are in the middle of the plane sandwiched between a very angry General Pete Wolf and his troops, and the unmentionable rock band seated in front of us. Alice gives me a 'Don't get involved' look. I don't need to, my work here is done, I think, reflecting on how effective my Maoist guerrilla tactics have been: stealth attack then retreat. A peanut whistles by my ear followed by a spit bomb. At Heathrow they will still be at it in the baggage reclaim. June 1994, I reflect to myself, and I am surrounded by rock 'n' roll cliché. It's only taken me less than 18 months to become one myself. It will have to get worse before it can get better. And it does.

14

Jesus, this is Iggy

July 1994. Garry Glitter is the surprise hit of the World Cup, when he performs 'Rock 'n' Roll Part 2' in Chicago. Stone Temple Pilots are number one in the US albums chart, while in the UK it's Ace of Base.

New York, very late night/early morning. Midsummer, suffocating heat. The telephone rings old style – ding a ling, ding a ling – shocking us out of our hard-won sleep. I lean across Alice and pick up the noisy intruder.

'Hey, Jesus, why didn't you call Genie Baby soon as you arrived?'

'It's 4.30 in the morning,' I respond, ever the stickler for protocol.

'I know, Jesus, and you're awake, so I'm coming straight over.'

Gene Horowitz arrives at the hotel half an hour later. Alice groans.

Gene Horowitz is a lively fish; his entire life is one long, self-indulgent free jazz solo.

'Have you ever considered taking heroin? I ask, as Gene runs the voodoo down. 'It would really calm your nerves and I hear it's terribly popular in England right now.'

I like Gene a lot; I met him just over a year ago when the Auteurs first played in America. He claims to be employed in some way by our US record company, but I just can't imagine anyone paying this guy money *and* having to see him every day. In reality (within the limitations of the relationship between reality and Gene Horowitz) I think everyone at the record company is too frightened to tell Gene that he doesn't actually work for them. Maybe that's what I like about Horowitz: he puts the wind up people something rotten. An ultra-kinetic cross between *The Gong Show* host Chuck Barris and Robert Walker Junior, with the schmooze button of a younger, hipper Rodney Bingenheimer. I'm also looking forward to mixing him up with my band. Gene is a kind of anti-Chalker; he talks about 'doing it with dudes', while Chalker chirrups on about 'mod birds with big knockers'. Gene calls me (and, for that matter, everybody else) Jesus. Chalker calls me the gaffer or boss. California, Crawley; never the twain, etc.

We're playing two nights in New York, at the tiny Mercury Lounge on the Bowery. The start of our latest American Tour. I've been off to 'Philly' for the day to 'hang' with Gene and his 'buddies'. See, I still love America. We get back to New York for the gig and the heat is searing. The sidewalk's molten and you lose litres of fluid as soon as you even think of moving. I vowed before this tour to behave myself. To try and keep a lid on the mind games, the manipulation, the self-sabotage. Hooking up with GH immediately was probably not the best thing to do. I am a human hand grenade and the prickly heat is tickling my loose little pin. Someone says something in the dressing room before the show – a perceived slight – and I am up and at 'em. Seconds later, and I have hurled a broken beer bottle indiscriminately into a crowd of strangers. Lies, deceit and broken promises all round. I am acting, as the Yanks would say 'like a jerk'.

We are a well-oiled machine of rock, with a smooth sophisticated gear system capable of many subtle dynamic shifts. The set is the usual mixture of songs from the new album, songs from *New Wave* and a brand new one called 'Light Aircraft on Fire'. After the show I'm out in the audience with Gene. After the bottle incident the band are giving me a wide berth; also I am quite ashamed of my behaviour. Gene, Gene, the networking machine.

'Hey, Jim! Jimmy! How ya doin'?' Gene beckons the little fella over.

The little guy is Iggy Pop.

'Hey, Iggy, what did you think of the Auteurs?' *Christ Almighty, Gene, don't ask Iggy Pop what he thinks of my band.*

'Yeah, Auteurs are cool,' says Iggy, smiling at me. 'And the electric cello,' Iggy continues, smile widening to the front cover of *Lust for Life*, 'is really cool.' *Ahhrggg no! Iggy, you fucking twat. The electric cello is not really cool. Every group in England has got a fucking electric cello. The Cellist's not like the Ashetons, you know. Or James Williamson. If he heard the guitar solo on 'Search and Destroy' he'd think it was rubbish. He doesn't understand us, Iggy. He's the anti-you. He's just waiting for someone to pay him more money, then he's off. Oh God, he's probably going to end up playing for you. It's all about me, Iggy, not him. Me. I wrote the fucking songs. He probably can't even remember the names of the fucking songs, let alone what any of them are about. Besides, Iggy, do you think he knows anything about you? Me, me, me. I've got all your albums, even* Party, *and you stand before me and tell me that the electric cello is cool. Oh Iggy.*

'Really cool,' reiterates the still beaming Iggy.

'Cool,' I parrot back. Hopeless.

The pioneers always go west. The US record company – Keith Wood – got it right when they said that this album and the song they have 'gone to radio' with, 'Lenny Valentino', could do well in America. In the weeks leading up to our American tour 'Lenny V' gets more and more ads on commercial/alternative radio. MTV is also using the song all over its terrible programme roster. Now if I can just resist the urge to throw spanners into the machinery along the way then, who knows, everything could work out. We wend our way down the east coast and play sold-out shows to rapturous audience response. But I don't travel well, and I don't like the ease with which the band can turn in a good show, and I don't like the meeting and greeting, and I don't like my behaviour, and I don't like half my band, and I don't like the album I am promoting, and I don't like the flights, and I don't like the heat, and I don't like what's happening behind my back in England, and I don't like the moments of camaraderie. The moral of the story is to never leave the house. But still the pioneers go west.

Does it play in Peoria? *You must be fucking joking, sunshine; it doesn't, and we are*. As the evangelists bluster away on the tour bus radio, we bluster away in the empty halls of the Midwest. Cleveland: attendance 20, capacity 800. Detroit: attendance 17, capacity 950, and on it goes. Now I'm a cowboy, a lonesome cowboy. Local radio stations give away free tickets for our shows to college kids who just want to get wasted on 'brewskis'. A week of demoralising poor attendances until we emerge from the dust bowl to play to a decent-sized audience in Chicago, where we get back onto the grip and grin circuit. I'm becoming a schmooze junkie getting a cruel kick out of the obsequious masochism of the various radio pluggers and record company execs who grasp at my clammy paws. And with each handshake 'Lenny Valentino' continues to thrive in a parallel universe, picking up more radio ads as we play to decreasing numbers.

A week later Alice and I wander up to Chinatown in the aftermath of our final show in San Francisco. Bad-vibe San Francisco, at the end of July. The tour has probably been successful in commercial terms, but my psyche has been ravaged and my body is ruined. I am inert. Completely poleaxed by my fear of flying. I shovel the woeful concoction of seeds, berries, hummus and fresh fruit – what passes for breakfast in California – around my oversized plate. I have an announcement to make: that I shall not be flying back to London today as planned, or for that matter at any time in the near future. Having once again asserted my independence, I then have to plead with Alice to stay on in San Francisco with me. (While being single-handedly responsible for visionary artistry, I am almost useless in all other practical aspects of life.) She looks doubtful for a moment but then brightly says we will make a holiday of it. Possibly a very long holiday. In bad-vibe San Francisco.

'So you're sure you can't get on the plane today,' says Manager Tony wearily. 'Well I'll try and reschedule the recording session, but Albini's a busy man . . .' Ah, the recording session. I first met Steve Albini when we played at the Metro in Chicago a week earlier. Steve Albini: a Cecil B. De Milne chariot race of attitude, skewering polemic and Polaris broadside. A rock 'n' roll oracle with the dial marked HIGHLY SUBJECTIVE hot-wired to full on. Man, he's even 70 per cent right about half his bullshit. I like Steve Albini from the off. He's also one of the five greatest recording engineers ever. Ever. But fuck all that, I'm on 'holiday'. Steve Albini can wait.

My first holiday for years. I loathe holidays – they're not for me – but I do my best to put a game face on. Every morning as

Frampton Comes Alive – pop weekly dies.

(*Above right*) Early publicity photo in Kensal Green cemetery. Original Auteurs line up. Left to right: Alice Readman, Luke Haines, Glenn Collins.

Improbable demand from defunct *Select* magazine.

Nouvelle vague 93.

First album cover: author with sheet wrapped around head.

Second album cover.

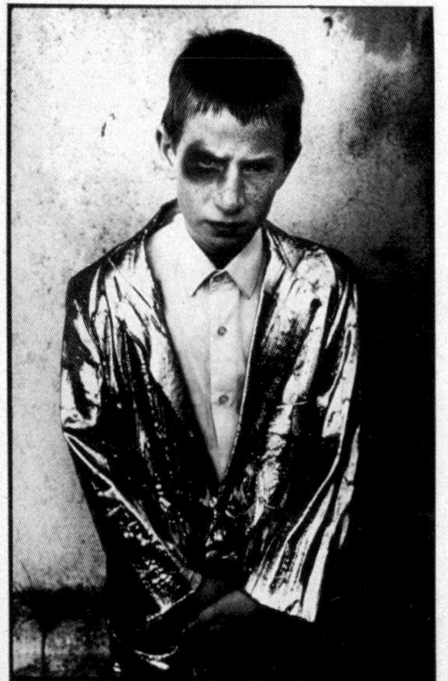

Murder Park period. Alice and Singer looking pleased with themselves. Cellist and drummer share a body bag and discuss.
(*Overleaf*) Luke Haines models proto Dennis Waterman/terror chic look – Munich Olympic stadium, 1996.

we wake in our ridiculous, opulent and beyond-our-means hotel, Alice gently enquires as to when we shall be flying home.

'Soon. I just need a few more days,' I offer. We catch trams and look at dolphins and seals (and move to a cheaper hotel). I stare at a walrus as it clambers up on the jetty and then uselessly plops back into the sea, repeating this movement over and over again. I stare at the beast intently. *I will engage with nature. Become one with nature*. Nope. Sixes and sevens, I'm afraid, all fingers and thumbs. SF is a dirthole of a town. The libertarian California farsightedness is invidious. For every trained sushi chef, hipster and raunchy cowboy, there are five dead-eyed ragamuffins who will cut you into ribbons. The brotherhood of eternal hatred is alive and well out there on the streets of San Francisco. Plus on the jukeboxes of the bars on Mission Street they have Pulp records but no Auteurs. Shithole-dwelling bastards.

The days become a week, and a week becomes two weeks, then at the beginning of the third week I steel myself. Alice books our flight home for the next day.

It's a beautiful day to fly. Well, as much as it can be. By now SF has become intolerable and even death in the skies is preferable to prolonging our stay. The flight is empty so we upgrade. I fix on the beauty in the aisle a couple of rows down; she will be my talisman. God would not dream of taking her. As we prepare for take-off the guy in the nearside seat clocks my anxiety.

'Nervous flyer, huh?'

'Ahuh,' I croak back. *Septic nosy parker*.

'Don't worry, I can guarantee that you'll be fine.'

I realise I have to play my part in his game, so in the hope of putting the conversation out of its misery as soon as possible, I politely ask how he can be so sure of our safe journey.

'Three years ago I was on a private jet that crashed in Delaware. Six passengers killed. I'm the sole survivor. Statistically the chances of me being involved in another accident are minimal,' he deadpans.

I want to worship the holy fool, kiss him on the mouth and wash his goddamn feet. My Meher Baba. My Maharashi Yogi. My Reverend Jim Jones. I will follow him to the end of the earth, and I will drink the Kool-Aid.[22] I catch the liquor lady's attention and greedily order a couple of vodkas. I gleefully pop a Mogadon and take an extra one for luck – though I no longer need it. This is gonna be the greatest flight in the world. Goodnight, night ladies and gentlemen. It's been swell.

Hours later, and I intuitively wake to hear the captain's announcement: 'Due to a technical fault we shall be making an emergency landing at Newark. I shall give you an update as soon as we have more information. In the meantime please fasten your seat belts.' Within half an hour we are just hundreds of feet above the ground. As we come in to land I can see the flashing lights of the fire engines and ambulances rushing along the runway trailing our landing.

My guru turns to me and nervously announces, 'This doesn't look too good.'

Sometimes words just fail me. But the combined effect of the alcohol and the Mogadons is too strong, and I lurch back into oblivion before the wheels hit the tarmac. 1994 is the year in which I age a decade.

[22] When over 900 followers of the Reverend Jim Jones take their own lives at the People's Temple in Guyana, they are instructed to drink Kool-Aid laced with deadly poison. What the murder/suicide victims were in fact drinking was grape Flavor Aid – laced with cyanide and valium – an entirely different product.

15

Loose horse

August 1994. Wet Wet Wet Greatest Hits *is number one in the UK album chart. Whigfield keeps the home fires burning for novelty pop with 'Saturday Night'. Slade 2 (minus Noddy Holder and Jim Lea) continue to make a decent living by playing universities and the European festival circuit. In Camden's Dublin Castle The Selector play a headline show.*

The recording studio is a vacuum. You can leave your drugs and your ego at the door. This place is a monastery. Man, I wish I'd just locked that studio door when I started recording *New Wave* back in '92 and never set foot in the real world again. Outside, the morons are gaining the whip hand. Inside, the band is working with Steve Albini. The session has been rescheduled due to my being marooned in San Francisco. After this we will be embarking on a European tour. A tour that I am dreading. The American is on trial though he doesn't know it – I have to keep some things to myself. You see, I need to know if he can cut it, if he's all he's cracked up to be. I can report that Steve Albini is most certainly all he is cracked up to be. We were five and now we're back to four, Steve Walker has once again been jettisoned after the US tour; he'll be back soon though, as a thorn in the side of the salarymen. The band, more harmonious than ever, are scheduled to cut two tracks with the Yank. Two tracks in two days. Then, if *I* like what we've recorded, we'll stay with Albini and record the album next year.

The songs 'Everything You Say Will Destroy You' and 'New Brat in Town' are wounded hungry ogres. It must be the weed, man, cos these two groaners are now monstrously slow, Black Sabbath 'Master of Reality' stoner tempo. We're getting way out of step, and I fucking love it. Rockford's breeze-block drum battalion pounds away dumb and doomleaden in the foreground, while the Cellist, now switched to a broken Korg organ under Albini's tutelage, has become the devil-may-care commander of a squadron of Stuka dive-bombers. Alice plunks through this sonic graveyard of malevolence and temper, solid as any member of Spector's Wrecking Crew. And me? Well I just hiss a path through the fucking songs, occasionally whacking off the old Hofner guitar for a bit of feedback or just filling a skeletal chord here and there. It's loose, it swaggers, and it does not give a shit.

Albini, as well as recording this holy dissent, busies himself by seeing how high the studio cat likes to be thrown in the air – frightening the record label and management – and paying extravagant and unselfconscious compliments to any passing ladies. 'Man, you smell good,' he remarks sweetly to Alice before setting his feet on fire.

Outside, what I first thought was a nasty dose of spring flu now, come summer, looks like it could become an epidemic. But I don't care, because I'm wise and I'm safe in here. I also suspect that I have found an ally in Steve Albini. By God, I need one. I'm a loose horse; my rider fell off at the second hurdle. I gallop across the track, veering this way and that. Unlike my other four-legged friends I am unencumbered by some halfwit jockey sitting astride me, shouting and thrashing away.

Everyone loves the sound of the new tracks – Albini, the record company, even me. Let the fools outside pursue their course. In time they will fall. Loose horse crosses the finishing line first but does not win the race.

16

Old Woman

Throughout summer 1994 the NME *prints a weekly fantasy football-style league table for bands, based on chart positions, reviews, etc. Readers can pick band members for a fantasy group and buy or transfer other members. Completely of its moment and utterly at odds with anything going through my mind at the time, it now aptly demonstrates my predicament. There are three league tables of players: the first valued at three to four million pounds each, the second two million upward, and the third valued between one and one a half million. Which is where I sit, for the duration, moving neither up nor down at the top of the third league. Between a rock and a hard place.*

The old woman in my head who sifts through the files that contain the memories that fill these pages needs a rest. So, as we reach an approximate halfway point in proceedings, why not let the old dear put her feet up for a few minutes as we examine that thing they call Britpop. We have to do it at some point – why put off the inevitable?

The rat in my kitchen: Britpop. At first it was something I only noticed late at night, when, after turning on the light, there would be a scuffling sound and a black shape with a hideous tail would dart across the floor into the cover of darkness or hide underneath the fridge. Foolishly I thought it would go away, but the fucker bred. Soon I could see rats in the daylight, sometimes patrolling together two or three at time. Every sound would cause my ears to prick up, and I would turn my head Terminator-style to where it emanated. I would stand rigid, staring into some dark corner looking for movement. Traps? Well I tried glue traps only to wake in the morning and witness a trail of ratty footprints but no stuck rat. Sometimes I would lie awake convinced I could hear the sound of squeaky rat laughter mocking me. This invasion of vermin was sending me off my rocker.

I have already dealt with the 1992–3 stirrings of Britpop and the death of Kurt Cobain, so here to provide a little background to the monstrous highs and woes of the proceeding chapters I take a look at the British music scene of 1994 and 1995. This account will of course be nothing other than highly subjective.

The fact that Britpop happened is incontestable; that it reached some kind of cultural plateau 1995–7 is a fallacy. Having laid the foundations, post-Suede and -Auteurs, the majority of the perpetrators of what would erroneously be seen as the first wave of Britpop – Oasis, Elastica, Gene and Sleeper – were signed up by record companies in mid- to late '93, after the relative mainstream success of Blur and Suede and the burgeoning commercial success of Pulp and, you guessed it, the Auteurs.

It should be noted that none of the above initially wanted any association with Britpop – no one wants to be part of someone else's scene – apart from those habitual bandwagon jumpers Blur. *Parklife* is nothing if not a masterclass in media complicity.

Radiohead then, the ones that got away untarnished. At the time of their first album – just after the Auteurs debut – this lot were certainly being prodded with the Britpop tickling stick. Live, however, Radiohead were – and this is pre the band's hand-wringing-conspiracy-theorising-meta-peacenik phase – rapidly turning into that most heinous of creatures: a heavy rock outfit, fright-wig and all. One wrong turn and it would have been into the valley of the Tygers of Pantang for good. But, with delicious irony, the Special Relationship came to the aid of our pals from Oxford: America. At the end of 1993, when the second-wave record company feeding frenzy of post-Suede and -Auteurs bands had begun, 'Creep' was finally a big hit single in the US. Radiohead did what Oasis, Blur, Suede and Pulp failed to do – break America. More importantly, they also won themselves a Britpop immunity card.

There were two fundamental insurmountable problems with Britpop. Firstly the term itself. Can you say it out loud without a twinge of embarrassment? Can you even think it without a slight shudder? Typically thought up by some lance corporal halfwit, possibly unaware that the term had been used before, to refer to that pre-Beatles milky light entertainment pop with a Norrie Paramour orchestral arrangement that used to clog up the hit parade on wet Sunday nights in the winter of 1960. Not half as good as I've just made it sound. The other problem is America. For British record companies it is vital that their acts sell in the States, the biggest market in the world. Bear in mind when I ask the following question that the entire music industry was complicit with the media in its attempt to mass-market Britpop. How on earth do you sell something called *Britpop* to the United States of America?

By 1995, in the more mundane universe than is my own, more

and more bands become unwittingly embroiled in Britpop. Pulp are up to their necks in it; the Boo Radleys, who have been around for years, gamely play along. Nasty. What seemed like a low-level illness has turned into a modern-day Black Death: Powder, Marion, Echobelly, Menswear, Kula Sh— Not yet. I can't bring myself to write it. Perhaps later, if it is strictly necessary. The big fish have nowhere to swim but in the little pond, and that's where Britpop does its real damage. The Oasis–Blur chart scrap of the summer of 1995 is little more than a battle of who can shout the loudest. An easy concept to grasp, but the most negative effect of these shenanigans is that, like the futile attempt to sell Britpop to the Yanks, the media and the record companies are once again deep within each other's pockets. English rock is from here on in forced to flagellate itself in subservience to the fallen angels of light entertainment. Nothing will ever be the same again. I pick up my broom, and sweep up my marvellous little emporium, and wonder how long I can put off a takeover.

The retelling of modern history has a habit of unnecessarily tying up loose ends. I shan't bother. If I see a nice neat knot I shall untie it and let the fucker hang loose; there is no parallel story of a political party putting on new shoes and dancing its way into Number 10, funded all the way by the Bluetones' early hits. In fact, by summer 1996, Oasis excluded, the public have generally lost interest in music. No clearer evidence of this can be provided than the malign chorus of 'Three Lions' bawled out endlessly in pubs throughout the land as England get knocked out of the European Nations Cup finals. As terrace chants go, 'Football's coming home . . .' is hardly up there with Chelsea's early 70s bootboy mantra 'We hate humans'.

*

Let's leave it there for now; it's inevitable that we will come across more Britpop as we go on. Time to wake the old woman up. *Did you have a nice rest, dear? I've made you a nice pot of tea, and I've brought you up a plate of biscuits. I'm afraid there's another filing cabinet of memory to sift through. Now go to the letter N. N for nadir. If you need anything else, just give me a shout.*

17

Psychopathology across Europe, or brick budgerigar part two

September – October 1994. Oasis are everywhere in September, most noticeably at the top of the album charts with their debut LP. In October the three surviving Beatles meet up, to re-record an old John Lennon demo. At the Grammies Frank Sinatra wins a lifetime achievement award. Dummy *by Portishead is released.*

Middlesex Hospital, central London. October 1994. The old fellow in the bed next to me went to sleep with both feet. He now appears to have lost a foot overnight. I stare unselfconsciously at the bandaged stump on the end of his right leg as my body slowly rouses itself out of unnatural, anaesthetised sleep. Oh yeah, I'm on the amputee ward. I woozily lift my head and manage to catch a glimpse of my own dogs, which, though both heavily bandaged and numb, are apparently still attached to the end of my legs. Just. A cheery nurse pushing the drug trolley pulls up at the end of my bed. Before I can begin piecing the events of the last few weeks together, I am given morphine and Valium. Lovely. It must have been a good night.

So, with no spare rooms at the inn, I am dumped in with the soon-to-be-limbless for the next two weeks. The higher powers in the hospital consider me to be mentally sturdy enough to cope with the acute bleakness of my new temporary home. The higher powers are wrong. By the third week of my incarceration I have been moved to a grim ward at the top of the hospital which seems to be used as some sort of state-subsided skip for the capital's homeless street drinkers, all of whom are knocking very loudly at death's door. I spend the week trying to block out the sound of the moron in the opposite bed, who when he is not throwing up blood uses every waking hour to aggressively shout inane questions at me. Unsurprisingly the number of visitors I get tails off during this week in purgatory – must be the company I'm keeping.

Dues paid and judgement passed I spend the fourth and final week of my sojourn in a pleasant enough ward where the only sociopath is me. Lovely Alice – long-suffering Alice, my little Florence Nightingale, who has visited me every day – manages to blag a wheelchair (a trickier task than you would think) so I can be wheeled out to the nearby One Tun pub on Goodge Street. More and more visitors come to take me out. Four or five Guinnesses in the alehouse, as much as my bladder can take (wheelchairs and pub toilets don't mix), and I'm back to the ward for a couple of Valiums and a damned good night's nod. The hospital even has a payphone on wheels, from which I imperiously conduct interviews with the *Melody Maker* and the *NME*, keeping an anxious world informed of my travails.[23] Eventually the hospital has enough

[23] Ostensibly, these interviews are to promote an album of unlistenable remixes known as *Auteurs Versus Musique*, two slabs of vinyl containing six fuck-awful, seizure-inducing, amateurish meanderings through the world of digital distortion. Only the terminally friendless could possibly be interested in this crock

of my larks and I am discharged to recover at home. I've almost forgotten that I had a different life, before the institutionalisation, which I have come to enjoy. Man, it's good to have a routine . . . Ah well, I guess all good things must come to an end.

The reason for my stay: both ankles badly broken, my right heel smashed to smithereens and a suspected fracture in my lower spine. All as a result of an Icarus plummet from a 15-foot wall onto unforgiving concrete in the unforgiving Spanish seaside resort of San Sebastián. I am taken to the local hospital, where a quack insists that I have sprained my ankles and I should really try to walk. My failure to do so prompts him into taking an X-ray of my spine which reveals a small fracture of the vertebrae. The miracle healer recommends that I fly home to London immediately and go straight to hospital.

Back home I try and crawl around hoping that by the end of the weekend the pain and swelling in my ankles will recede. It doesn't. By Monday morning I look like I have a balloon on the end of each leg, so I check myself into hospital. The good news is that the spinal fracture detected in the Spanish hospital is not detected

---

of cack. To no ones's surprise the album receives ecstatic reviews. The whole wonky endeavour has been dreamt up by myself, David Boyd and Tony Beard. *Musique* receives a teeny tiny fee, and I bag the all-important publishing, which is nice, because the record actually sells in the States. In 1975, after the uber-cynical yet super-selling *Sally Can't Dance* album, Lou Reed followed up with *Metal Machine Music*, four sides of guitar feedback that almost ruined his career. 'If you listen to all four sides of it then you're even dumber than I am,' quoth Lou. *MMM* is worth getting on vinyl for the sleeve alone. The back cover features some electronic circuit bullshit that Lou copied straight out of a hi-fi magazine and the great quote 'My week beats your year.' *Auteurs Versus Musique* is really just a chance to indulge my *Metal Machine* fantasies.

here. Good old Blighty, the finest healthcare in the world, etc. The ankles, mind you, are fucking kindling. But I'd kind of guessed this. So, checked into the toy factory, I am wheeled off to be mended and rethreaded by the toymaker, along with all the other broken toys. I wake up midweek, held together with Sellotape and glue. The operation went well, says the toymaker, but, given the nature of the fractures and the possibility of spinal trauma, 'There is a chance that you may not walk again.' The words buffer against my brain a few times, ricochet off around the room then make one final pass at my brain before I bat them away. Unnecessary mosquitoes of reality that, right now, can do me no good whatsoever. *Well*, I think to myself, *at least the voices in my head have stopped yabbering, and the ghosts that have been plaguing me over the last few months have been vanquished*.

The European tour that begins in September '94 and ends . . . well, we now know where it ends. The tour that as fast as I whittle dates off our booking agent adds more dates onto actually starts with a preamble in Los Angeles, where we are to spend two days making a video for 'New French Girlfriend' before flying straight to Munich to start the tour proper. The record company has flattered me into doing this video for a song I am bored with and don't want releasing as a single by telling me how much the director, Kevin Kerslake, wants to work with me and how he's such a fan that he's practically paying us, blah blah blah. Flattery of this kind never fails.

The record company even tells me that Kerslake directed Nirvana's 'Heart Shaped Box' video, which I am fond of. He didn't; Anton Corbijn did. Ignorance on my part. I didn't check, too busy basking in the golden glow of flattery. None of which matters, as Kerslake is a decent, funny guy. Off we pop to LA to tart up my big song about nothing at all with a promo video about not much at all. The band listlessly mime instruments and loll about on wasteland within sight of LAX airport. An Amazonian model pounds up and down a makeshift catwalk while a pretty girl wearing a Bretagne shirt, a beret and – get this – a string of onions round her neck tries to hold my hand as I lip-sync very badly. All the while Alice staring daggers at me. During a break from shooting a member of the film crew mutters wearily but audibly, 'Just another English band. Another. Fucking. English. Band.' I'm sick of promoting this stale album, playing the same twenty songs ad nauseam. At another time I may have bothered taking the naysayer down a peg or two but my heart's just not in it, and he may well be right.

We are jet-lagged when we arrive in Munich after the long flight from LA. I don't mind though. After the boredom of shooting the promo for 'New French Girlfriend' and the ennui of the video itself, my mind is occupied by thoughts of the new album. Working title *Uber Hate*. As we drive through Bavaria I can picture the words in huge embossed Teutonic lettering on the album sleeve. My mind wanders. *Auteurs Uber Alles could look good as well. Oh God, have I really entered my rock 'n' roll fascist stage so soon?* Rock music just can't get enough of those naughty Nazis. Ever since the Fabs rocked their Gestapo-rent-boy-meets-hairdresser-from-the-Wirral look at their Reeperbhan peak, rock 'n' rollers have been beating a tireless path to the Führer Bunker. Keith Moon and Viv Stanshall wandering round Soho dressed as German officers. Punk and the 'Situationist' use of the swastika. Throbbing Gristle and the arch, art provocateur use of Nazi talisman. Don't worry too much about it; the mystical lie of the Nazi death camp, *Arbeit macht frei* – Work shall set you free – is unlikely to be applied by anyone in a rock group. Possibly a boy band, but that is a more motivated strain. It's just that musicians like to see themselves as outsiders and outlaws. Trouble is, most outsiders are not that successful.

Adolf was briefly successful in his mentalist Reich, and in the long term achieved mythical status as the Bogeyman chief of the twentieth century. Rock music would definitely like some of that. First rock star? Oh please. Mark Antony, Brutus, Wilde, Paganini . . . The list could go on. We just can't help ourselves. This fixation on Nazi iconography is adolescent, deeply stupid and immature. Just like a lot of great rock 'n' roll. The morning after our first gig on the never-ending European tour, I conform to type. Jet-lagged and hungover I find myself trudging around former concentration camp Dachau, just outside Munich. *Just another fucking English band*. I listen to the German tour guide apologise to a party of schoolchildren on behalf of his ancestors for their part in the Holocaust. I can't take any more of this, though I'm not the first person to think that in this awful place. I stock up on death-camp knick-knacks from the gift shop and wander off, through the chocolate box Black Forest scenery, hoping to hail a taxi back into the city. A few hundred yards down the road and I pass a Burger King. I don't stop. I'm not hungry.

I first started hearing the voices on the last American tour. By the time we get to Cologne the voices are in full bloody chattering mode. Then the 'ghosts' arrive. As if there are not enough people in our touring party, my brain has decided to conjure up small apparitions that float horizontally near the ceiling of every new hotel room. Luckily, I am not afflicted by a belief in mumbo-jumbo, so I am mostly aware that I am undergoing some kind of neurological malfunction. By the third or fourth episode of the apparition show, I start to think that this is a normal occurrence. I'll deal with it some other time, get myself rewired. Alice, however, realises that I am going fucking nuts. Poor sweet Alice, having to share her hotel room with me and my invisible pals in the air. At least they don't talk too much.

The voices and the ghosts are a not entirely positive sign of things to come. Our touring party has polarised. The four-piece unit which had been getting on famously at the last studio session has now fragmented again, all because of the reintroduction of the hapless Chalker. I take this fractious split as insubordination and a personal affront. Alice and I keep to ourselves and Chalker is immediately made a pariah. The four-man road crew are a self-contained unit, and the Cellist and Rockford engage in some weird, vaguely irritating fake homoerotic monkey business. To make their pseudo bumboy antics worse, the pair have smuggled matching Bickerton foldaway bikes on board the tour bus. It's all part of some cock-eyed plan to make this endless march through Europe something more than just a tour – something more like a biking holiday. For just the two of them. Oh what joy for the rest of us. It's all so un-Iggy, it just makes me want to weep. At every pit stop the horrible little machines are unfolded, and the Cellist and the Drummer climb astride their dwarf bikes and buzz round and round the tour bus, like fruit flies mating. The road crew try to destroy the Bickertons, crashing heavy amplifiers on top of them in the back of the splitter bus, all to no avail – those bastard Bickerton bikes are indestructible.

Hamburg is the last night of the German leg of the tour. So far we have engaged in the usual Brit-band-in-the-Fatherland antics: I have played all the gigs wearing my First World War fighter pilot hat and a German office's three-quarter-length coat – a gesture of unification. At motorway service stations we open the windows and doors of the bus and treat the locals to the stereo blasting out the theme to *The Great Escape* – a gesture of non-unification. (Rock 'n' roll is all about embracing the contradiction.) Still, no recognition, not even a hint. Perhaps the passing travellers know that it's best not to give us the attention we crave. Or perhaps *The Great Escape* doesn't get shown very often on German television. The crew pack the last of the gear into the back of the vehicle. Alice, Mikey and I sit up front. Round and round go the Bickertons. This is an extremely uncool scenario. As the Cellist and the Drummer come into view on their millionth circuit of the bus, I exchange glances with Mikey and Alice and we all three smile sweetly at the cycling pests, who are now performing stunts like little children, happy to have their parents' blessing. Sometimes on a long tour wit is best kept in reserve, to be used sparingly and only when strictly necessary. We keep smiling at the uncool fools, but it's a piss-poor show.

The voices can only be silenced by alcohol and dope. If I drink and smoke enough then I'm not awake long enough to be bothered by my hotel-room apparitions. It's obviously a vicious circle, but, right now, both commodities are essential to me. The dope has become problematic. European motorway police have become even more tenacious in their pursuit of English tour buses rammed full of drugs. We know by now that we will only get a fine but it's a drag getting the stuff confiscated all the time. We hit Amsterdam and stock up. Rockford, a natural in these matters, has an ingenious idea. We will post as much dope as is required on to the venues we are playing and on to some of the hotels. Fantastic. We now have a crap international drug smuggling operation on the go.

Endless Europe and endless chatter, some from real people, some from imagined people. Germany, Sweden, Denmark, then back to Holland for a couple of shows and down to Belgium. We have played in Brussels once before and I hadn't expected to be asked back: on an early European sortie for the first album, we ended up playing an industry-only bash in Bruges. Unfortunately there was a queue of around a hundred willing-to-pay fans who the venue and record company would not let in. In an uncharacteristic moment of Clashesque doing-it-for-the-kids altruism, I announced that we would not play unless the real fans were allowed in. For free. I was politely told that this would not be possible. I surmounted this obstacle by putting everyone on the guest list. All hell broke loose, and everybody lost their temper. More characteristically I went off on one, being as obnoxious as possible to the record company, haranguing their guests and the hapless support band. We arrived back in London to be told by Virgin UK that the Belgian record company would no longer be promoting the album. To their credit Hut were amused by the whole debacle. Major record labels, like the police and government intelligence agencies, take a perverse pleasure in the self-defeating pursuit of one-upmanship against the people you are supposedly working with. The gig, by the way, was rotten. I drunkenly slobbered and drooled over the microphone, and hurled abuse at members of the audience who I singled out and pompously denounced as freeloaders. A large section of the room collectively shuffled a few steps back into the dimly lit bar area, hoping that they – and I – would be swallowed up by the floor. I even managed to play the first three songs not noticing the plectrums stuck between the strings of my guitar.

It really is unpleasant for all concerned to find ourselves back once again, and it's no surprise that chaos ensues. To everybody's horror all the people involved in the last atrocity are present and correct. Initially I try hard to make amends with the Belgian record company people, and they seem willing. But the longer I have to hang around before going on stage, the more time I have to: a) replay the events of our last visit here over and over in my head, b) drink. The old wounds, it would appear, cannot be healed. Bad habits, once again, die hard and we have a rerun of last year's fiasco with the same result. By the end of the evening I have even managed to sack my own band. The next day, en route to France, the mood is black and vile. The workers have clearly had a secret post-gig hotel-room summit. Result: the spare parts are no longer talking to me. *Why the fuck are you lot still hanging around? Didn't I sack you all last night? Haven't you got homes to go to?*

The little packages bulging with clumps of skunky Dutch weed and lumps of hash winging their way through the French postal system have become an obsession. As soon as we reach the hotel Rockford and I casually enquire as to whether we have received any post. When we are told no we are left in a state of acute paranoia. To the promoters of the venues I deliver prolonged lectures on the workings of the French motorway police and the intricacies of the French mail system. Partly because I enjoy wasting their time and watching their eyes glaze over. Partly because I am losing my mind. Possessing crap dope in France is a pretty minor offence, but we are now dealing – albeit to ourselves. The Drummer and I half expect to be met by Interpol somewhere along the line. None of this is helping my fragile mental state, as the voices and apparitions make their presence felt. Perhaps I should be grateful, as no one else wants anything to do with me. One morning while posting some dope on to a hotel in Toulouse I also pop a postcard into the letter box, addressed to David Boyd, my A & R man at Hut Recordings:[24]

[24] DB archives all my missives and answerphone meltdowns for his own amusement. Sweet.

Dear Dave
Everything you touch turns to shit.
XLH

I don't remember writing that, I think to myself as the card falls irretrievably down the hole. I do, however, have a vague recollection of watching my disembodied hand scrawling the shapes that make up the words. At least now I have an excuse for my worsening behaviour. I can now claim that God, or some other external demon voice, told me to do it. Just like Peter Sutcliffe.

Only Alice is loyal to me, but even she cannot protect me from the ugly spirits, the nagging voices and the ghosts that are ever-present. *You lot still here*, I think, gazing at the backs of the heads of my sacked band. The king in exile, sat on his throne at the back of the tour bus, and the lost dogs in front, still hanging around waiting for me to throw them a bone. When William Burroughs accidentally killed his wife Joan in a drunken game of William Tell, he talked of being controlled by a malevolent force: 'the ugly spirit'. Recalling the tragedy Wild Bill said, 'I knew something awful was going to happen to me that day. I was walking down the street with tears streaming down my face. If that happens to you – *watch out, baby*.' Christ, imagine if Burroughs had to put up with Alan Ginsberg and Gregory Corso twatting about on Bickerton midget bikes. Shooting the missus would have been the tip of the iceberg.[25]

[25] As every schoolboy knows, Burroughs shot and killed his wife Joan in Mexico City in 1951. The William Tell act had been done before; this time however Burroughs was drunk on tequila and he missed the tumbler balanced on Joan's head, killing her immediately. The door that Joan was standing against is now apparently owned by Damien Hirst. Eventually Burroughs was found guilty of homicide in absentia and given a two-year suspended sentence.

San Sebastián, Basque country in northern Spain. The mood on the bus has lightened – people are once again talking to me. After the long and crushingly familiar trek through France everybody feels relieved to be in Spain. Everybody except me – *watch out, baby*. I lie on the bed in my hotel room and watch TV, manically changing channels, hoping to find a frequency capable of blocking it all out. The ghosts are spinning horribly out of control, and the voices are constantly goading and needling. The only way to stop this madness is to leave the hotel and find a bar to get drunk in. There is no show tonight, so I have my work cut out. I leave Alice to sleep. She says she will catch up with me later. She's concerned. She knows I've gone crazy. By early evening I have met up with the rest of the touring party. Everyone is here and the atmosphere is easy. We're all getting on and having a *good* time. I'm in my cups, chipper and dandy, and I'm gonna drink this seaside resort dry. *Watch out, baby*.

I wobble above the precipice. The list of tour dates still remaining blows across what is left of my mind like tumbleweed. Spain, Italy, back to France then on to Japan. At least now I know what I have to do. If I make the 15-foot jump then we continue. If I hobble myself then events will take a different turn. In the gloom of the early hours I can't even tell what I'm jumping down onto. Sand or concrete?

Concrete then. After the nanosecond of my descent I hear Alice shriek as I crumple on the deck. A sack of shit. Didn't make it then. Mikey, Big Neil and Chalker take the stairs down to me and carry my useless body back to the hotel as only waves of relief roll over me. Alice walks alongside us in stunned disbelief. Come morning I will not regret a thing. As I lie on the bed my body goes into shock. Alice covers me with more blankets as I shake uncontrollably. For the moment the booze has dulled the pain that, in a few hours, will render me bloody helpless, writhing and screaming on the bathroom floor. Soon I will sleep. The voices have gone, as have the ghosts. It's almost 3 a.m. Today, on 7 October 1994, I am 27 years old. Happy fucking birthday.

18

Uber hate

October–December 1994. Take That are number one in the UK singles chart followed by Pato Banton at the end of October. Nirvana's MTV Unplugged in New York *album is released. In November the Stone Roses release* Second Coming, *their second album, to gales of laughter. On 23 December Tommy Boyce, co-writer of so many of the Monkees' smashes, blows his brains out. The Christmas number one in the UK singles chart is 'Stay Another Day' by East 17.*

The man in the photograph is unwell. His eyes are bloodshot and bleary, his complexion sallow. On his chin there are the beginnings of a patchy, unkempt beard. His face is bloated by prescription medication. The tatty beige shirt, creased and dirty, might be taken as evidence that its occupier is not intent on impressing anyone in the outside world at any time in the near future. I am the man in the photograph, and the photograph is attached to the visa stapled inside my passport for a cancelled Japanese tour. Beneath the mugshot, which has my name beside it, I am required to state my occupation. The word that has been used, which apparently does this best is entertainer. Entertainer. Hahahaha.

It's a good joke for sure. What on earth kind of entertainer am I? I will have to wait to find out because right now, in the winter of '94, I'm down in the basement and I'm not going anyplace at all. *Watch out, baby.*

Against the backdrop of bloody civil war, paranoia about the new 'religion' of science and general lawlessness, Matthew Hopkin – self-appointed witch-finder general – carried out a two-year reign of terror in East Anglia. Between 1645 and 1647 Hopkin tried and put to death over 200 'witches'. What motivated Hopkin is not fully known, but he was without doubt a cruel and pious man who also made filthy lucre from the bounties he was paid. Like Hopkin, I too am a cruel and pious man. And, like Hopkin, I am searching out the unholy using pain. Pricking and needling, seeking out the mark of the supernatural. If I stab you and you don't feel a thing, then you're guilty. But if you feel the pain and you're lucky enough to survive, then I'll know that you're innocent. From now on, if you get it, it's going to hurt.[26]

The full idiocy of the era has yet to be felt. But I already loathe the brashness, the vicars-and-tarts-forced-jollity of the Blur–Elastica alliance. The head boy and head girl appear to be doing rather well for themselves. I had more of a *Carrie*-style ending in mind for the

[26] Hopkin's first witch hunt took place in Manningtree, a village close to Colchester in 1644. Nineteen 'witches' were hanged, and four more died from torture in prison. Hopkin would prick his suspect with a knife to find the point at which they felt no pain: the 'witch's spot', or the 'mark of the supernatural', from which the suspect would feed their familiar or demon. Blur's Damon Albarn hails from Colchester.

nauseating couple. Christ, I didn't mind this mob when they were all pretending to be little mod bands; now they're carrying on like they run the joint. Meanwhile, the Gallaghers' ascendancy is assured. By the end of the year the brothers' latest monstrosity of a single will be deemed such a momentous occasion that the thick-headed management of the *NME* will command every one of its toady writers to gush over it, taking up most of the singles review page. The song in question is called 'Whatever'. It sounds like the fucking Ruttles. It is cack. It will not be remembered. My hackles are up, and my puritanical streak is at the fore. In the basement of my Camden flat I rattle around between three dark rooms in my wheelchair, popping pills and not washing. If I look up from my window, I can see them blowing up the balloons outside. The first guests are arriving and the marquee has been up for months. I heard about the party a long time ago, when I was well. Soon it will be in full swing, but I won't be going. I'm not invited anyway.

I can go forward, and I can go back. But I cannot go up – to shuffle up two flights of stairs on my backside is, ahem, a drag – and I'm already down. I am the laird of the bedroom, the front room and the bathroom of the lowest quarters of the cramped Georgian house. In life as in art I am now of the downstairs class. Dostoevsky in *Notes from Underground*, the Lord Protector on wheels. Over the preceding months the voices had blocked out any chance of new songs coming to the fore. Now that the voices have gone I am free to write, though it will take a while. *Prick, prick, prick, stab, stab, stab*. Got to find the witch's spot. The first new songs 'Mace' and 'Uber Hate' are ugly, brutal meditations on rape and misanthropy. I'm clearly out of practice at this caper. If you're going to 'walk on the dark side of the street', as comedy Marty Diamond would have it, then you had better be good. You may not be entertaining, but make damn sure you are the best.

Judging from the whoops and applause from the marquee outside, the marching band and jugglers have already arrived. No need for another song-and-dance man. *Scratch, scratch, scratch, scrape, scrape, scrape.* Still searching for the witch's spot. Don't let the howls of pain put you off, you've got a job to do.

'Unsolved Child Murder' seems to arrive out of nowhere. Then I recall the source, an incident from my own childhood that has remained deep within the recesses of my memory until now: a child of maybe three or four years old who lived at the top of the road disappeared, it must have been Christmas 1972. The road I live in is built on a steep hill. The missing child's house is at the top of the hill. The child's name is Jamie. We are in suburban southern England, and I am five years old. Me and the other kids in the street didn't play with Jamie that much – he had rickets and his legs were often encased in calipers. As if this wasn't enough, he was a sickly child too. When we did play with him it was more out of duty than genuine fun. Then he disappeared. I remember gloomy afternoons in Jamie's house, sent to keep the missing boy's older sisters company. While my parents and other neighbours dropped by, silently helping and comforting Jamie's parents, we played in the room next door. Jamie's father was a doctor, and I clearly remember being unable to comprehend how something awful could happen when your daddy was a doctor – physician, heal thy offspring. Was the little boy abducted or did his weak body just give up against the onslaught of illness? I still don't know what happened.

Once 'Unsolved Child Murder' has written itself, I start channelling the nightmare bogeymen of 70s newsreel infamy, the nursery rhymes of my cosseted childhood: John Stonehouse, the Tory MP who faked his own death; Sandra Rivett, the nanny accidentally murdered by 'Lucky' Lord Lucan; the sub-post office killing spree of Donald Neilson the Black Panther; the kidnapping of Lesley Whittle; Peter Sutcliffe and the notorious ripper hoaxer Wearside Jack; the car bombings of the Angry Brigade; the plane hijackings of the PFLP; and the simultaneous suicides of the leading members of the Baader-Meinhof gang.

The devils are jumping out of the box. Even before the accident I knew that the songs of faded glamour and new French girlfriends were long gone; I just wasn't able to pluck the new material from the air. Now, confined to a wheelchair, I feel liberated, and the songs are imbued with a psychic subterranean claustrophobia: 'Land Lovers' is a meditation on amputation and espionage; 'Child Brides' a half-remembered tale of a late-eighteenth-century double suicide pact on the Norfolk Broads; and 'Dead Sea Navigators' a drinking song in honour of a childless itinerant couple who drift between seaside B & Bs with only their DTs and the mortal remains of their dear dead infant son, stored in a trunk, for company. The voices in my head that had nowhere to go have stopped nagging; now they just stream out of my pen into fully formed verses. I am my own amanuensis.

More songs appear on blank sheets of paper: 'Married to a Lazy Lover', a sickly prowl through domestic violence, obsession and alcoholism, and 'After Murder Park', the album's eventual title and sequel to 'Unsolved Child Murder', a three-way conversation between the missing child's parents, a medium and the voices from the other side. 'Lenny Valentino' seems a lifetime ago. I know I will no longer be vying for chart positions with Pulp. There are pros and cons to most things.

By 1647 various institutions had grown tired of Matthew Hopkin and his ilk, and Parliament saw fit to officially denounce witch-finding. There are conflicting reports as to Matthew Hopkin's demise. Some say that villagers turned on him and he himself was accused of witchcraft, and given the 'swim test'. He failed and did not drown. The mob took him away and he was put to death by hanging. A more prosaic report has Hopkin expiring in bed from consumption. Fuck that. I've been shuffling around in the basement for two months writing these psychotic episodes that I am now going to pass off as songs. The braying villagers outside my window can chance their arm if they like, but I am not going to expire in bed. By Christmas 1994 I can just about support myself on crutches. A modern miracle to confound medical science. I am now free to hobble, limp and stumble around my Camden Town locale, my walking sticks a pair of branding forks that I shake in anger at the burgeoning Brit populace. *Prick, prick, prick, stab, stab, stab. Watch out, baby.*

19

Horny

January 1995. In Select *magazine's writers' poll of the top 30 albums of the last year, Oasis are at number one. Blur's* Parklife *is at number two.* Dog Man Star *by Suede is at number eight.* His 'n' Hers *by Pulp is number 17, and the Auteurs'* Now I'm a Cowboy *is at number 21. 'Cotton Eye Joe' by Rednex is number one in the UK singles chart.*

The Great Hanshin Earthquake hits Kobe at 5.46 a.m. on Tuesday, 17 January 1995, measuring 7.3 on the Richter scale. There are no foreshocks, and the tremors last for 20 seconds. Over 6000 people – mainly in Kobe – lose their lives and more than 26,000 are injured. A large section of the spectacular Hanshin Expressway, a futuristic Fritz Lang flyover linking Kobe to neighbouring Osaka, is destroyed. The Kobe Earthquake, as it will come to be known outside Japan, is the country's worst natural disaster since the Great Kanto Earthquake of 1926, which claimed 140,000 lives. Tuesday, 17 January 1995. Having just completed a short tour of Japan, the Auteurs drag their tired bodies on board the 5 a.m. JAL flight from Osaka to London. We escape the earthquake by three quarters of an hour.

'When we see you on to stage, you remind us of Scott Walker,' says the earnest young journalist at the press conference, the morning after the first of two Tokyo shows. This man may be on to something. Something that no other journalist has ever or will ever pick up on.

'Are you the new Scott Walker?' he continues.

Before I can decide to either demur or agree with this ludicrous idea, another writer pipes up: 'Thom Yorke says that no one has attitude like Luke Haines.'

Does he mean this in a good way? I wonder to myself. The truth of the matter is: if they like you in Japan then they will talk you up something rotten, any lie to make their guests feel good. When they don't like you, then you simply don't exist. No bad words, no harsh critique, nothing. Ah what the hell. It's just good to be the centre of attention again.

However many mantraps, snares and kamikaze missions I thrust in the path of my career trajectory, some things are just meant to be, and I, like many others who have come before me, must pick up the gauntlet. It is now my turn to be big in Japan. This tour, quickly rescheduled after last year's accident, is turning out just swell. I am up on crutches full time. This is maybe not the best way to tour a country as initially shocking and strange as Japan – Tokyo is an all-out attack on the senses, a hectic neon overload – but no doctor's note is going to get me out of this.[27] In a moment of clarity I have decided that the best way of completing this short tour is to cut out the painkillers and the sedatives that are sapping my strength.

[27] If I cop out of the tour, there is a good chance I will be sued by the promoters.

I've also temporarily quit dope and alcohol. This happy temperance has two effects. Firstly, I now bound around – albeit with walking sticks – like a jolly Christian. I am actually going through withdrawal symptoms, and circuits which had long been shut down are now juddering into working order again. I am behaving more like David Thewlis' ranting Johnny character in *Naked* than the easy-going camper I think I've become – well, at least I'm happy. The second is that my libido has woken up and is about to come hurtling through the window. As our plane lands at Narita on 10 January 1995, a realisation dawns on me: I'm horny. Ladies of the Orient, you have been warned.

So we are bigger than the Beatles?[28] No. Bigger than the Walker Brothers? No. Well, perhaps bigger than Robyn Hitchcock. Anyway, all the shows are sold out in advance, and the Japanese fans go crazy: that is they clap politely and remain in their seats until the end of the gig, when they finally allow themselves to go nuts. I've loosened up – at least verbally – on this tour, and songs get long preambles. Between numbers I deliver lengthy monologues on anything that takes my fancy. Perhaps a non-English-speaking culture is not the best place to try out my new shtick, but the Japanese seem to have a knack for zeroing in on the gimmick: guitar shops sell more novelty miniature axes and tiny amps than is strictly necessary; gigs start at teatime, and alcohol is sold in vending machines on the street. Care for a ready-mixed Scotch mac? I figure that the more esoteric elements of Western culture shouldn't be too much of a problem. I'm still of course on heat.

By the time we hit the streets, in the early January evening after the first Tokyo show (it's only 7.30 p.m.), the fans waiting to greet

[28] The Beatles arrive in Japan on 29 June 1966. The Fab Four godhead changes Japanese culture for good.

us have become a frenzied mob. One of the girls in the mob is on a mission. She's a man-made vision, cannot be more than 18 years old. An Iggy Pop hard-on: plastic mac, red plastic trousers and, of course, plastic stilettos. She passes me a note, which I pocket, and disappears into the night. Here it is almost rude for fans not to bestow gifts upon their idols. We are all laden down with plastic dolls, home-made biscuits, CDs and offers of sexual congress. The next morning the Iggy Pop Hard-On girl is loitering in the hotel lobby. This time she speaks to me and introduces herself as Suki X. As Suki yabbers away in broken English, I notice an older guy loping around on the sofa 20 yards away. Suki tells me she has travelled far to see my group; she makes some flirty small talk and presses another letter into my hand. As she makes for the automatic doors she turns around and tells me she'll see me after tonight's show. Uh oh. I limp into the elevator thinking there's something wrong about all this. The elevator doors close for a few seconds, then reopen. Just in time for me to see through the glass frontage of the hotel that the older guy on the sofa is now walking down the street, and out of my vision, with Suki X.

The jet lag accrued from London to Tokyo is vicious. Nausea sets in at around midday, followed by exhaustion at around 5 o'clock – showtime. By late evening we are all raring to go. Sleep kicks in at around 1 a.m., followed by the rude waking of our fucked-up body clocks a mere few hours later at 4 a.m. For some reason this roughly coincides with the time that the hotel chooses to turn off the power – the lights and the television in our rooms at least – until 6.30 in the morning.

The evening of the second Tokyo gig and the 'New Scott Walker' is going on a bit. Maybe it's the sight of the lead singer coming on stage with a walking stick or the image of my locally acquired steamed-up National Health-style bins, but tonight the audience are not assimilating quite as well as I'd hoped. No problem. I cut the chat and the band kick in with 'Landlovers', my new song about amputation. After the performance the fans receive us outside and shower us with more gifts. It's quite touching, but there's the nagging doubt that there is nothing more to this than Japanese ritual. Suki X and her friend are nowhere to be seen. Her first note was a polite, flirty, welcoming introduction. I'd been thinking that the girl was an escort and the guy her pimp, but the second letter, a psychosexual rant full of references to self-harming, makes me think otherwise. This is what it must be like being in the Manic Street Preachers. After the hysterical mob have been dealt with, the promoters take us all out, band and crew, for a banquet, where we all laugh at stories of Oasis' recent visit here, and how they couldn't cope with Japanese food and had to spend their time skulking around in Burger King. We sneer at the unpleasant Manc peasants as we help make endangered species, some barely dead, extinct.

Nagoya: Suki and her pal have turned up again. Now there's some pretty frightening desperation going down. Her accomplice is not even bothering to be inconspicuous. Suki tells me that we are to run away to the mountains together, it's some kind of destiny. What a peach. I think of the beautiful mountain scenes on the bullet train journey from Tokyo. *Ah, Suki, if only things were different.* Then it falls into place. I'm being 'flirty fished'.[29] They're trying to recruit me; they're in a sect. The tall guy is her minder, she's the bait, and I'm the mark. I am of course insulted. Me of all people. I turn on my heel, pulling Alice out of harm's way and I don't look back once until I'm safely holed up in the bar. When I

[29] Method of recruitment used by cults, whereby pretty girl lures in possibly gullible young man with the promise of sexual favours.

tumble back into the hotel I book myself and Alice on to an earlier bullet train for the final show in Osaka. I have had it with these creeps, who will no doubt be waiting for me at the next destination. I ain't no cult cannon fodder. There's only room for one David Koresh around here, and that's me.

Osaka City is vast. A sensory overload of seemingly endless straight roads, steel, glass and neon skyscrapers, and row after row of street vendors and entertainers. The only thing I *really* notice is the earthquake protection grills on all the windows. Everything is happening in slow motion now; I must be in the thick of the jet lag. I walk down one of the endless straight roads in slow motion. We play a sweltering gig in a tiny basement club. I forget to remove my glasses before going on stage, and I steam up again. I play the first song in blindness and the kids go nuts for their myopic crippled messiah. After the show we go through the autograph and gift ritual in slow motion. Crazy Suki turns up again. Now I'm worried that she will exact some kind of vengeance upon Alice – she knows she can't get to me. Out of the mob she stretches her hand, persisting, still trying to tempt me. She tries to pass another letter to me in slow motion. I snatch it avoiding eye contact. Expedient measures.

The plane is chock-full of Japanese fashion students all Westernised up and excited to be on their way to London. They bob up and down in their seats with their stupid haircuts, dyed ridiculously, and their haven't-got-it-quite-right clothes, and I just think to myself, *You are the sweetest thing I've ever seen*. Only the dumbest, hardest heart could not fall in love or be totally envious of these kids, who have it all ahead of them. Then I turn my attention to Chalker, seated a few rows behind me. Chalker has definitely not got it all ahead of him. In the last letter that lovely Suki presented me with, she included, among some of her more outré sexual ramblings, a psychotic review of the Osaka gig. Steve Walker is sat quietly minding his own business, listening to his Walkman. Sometimes Chalker's stoicism in the face of downright hostility is a provocation in itself. The man is an immovable object who somehow represents the entire stuck-in-the-mud stupidity of the music industry.

'I've got a review that you're mentioned in,' I hiss, dragging him away from his Who tape. He reads the scrawled letter excitedly, anticipating his namecheck. I register his confusion as he realises the agitated state of the reviewer's mind, until he gets to the penultimate line: 'And please you should get rid of spare guitar player. He is useless.'

The 'spare' guitarist is crestfallen.

'It's the fans,' I console, 'who can be the harshest of critics. John Lennon found that out.'

Alice has just burst into tears. An understatement – she is weeping uncontrollably. The floodgates open the moment the plane stops moving on the tarmac at Heathrow. Everyone else is going home to a fresh face, one that may have even missed them. Alice lives and tours with a maniac, and she is now going back home with him. Maybe it's been the stress of the last few months, taking care of the wounded lunatic and acting as de facto band manager. (Tony is still very much our manager but I refused to swallow the cost and let him accompany us to Japan. For the last few months he has been sulking, and now he is busying himself with a couple of useless new acts. To punish, undermine and show him that he needs us more than the other way around, Alice and I take on some of the managerial side of things ourselves.) Or perhaps she senses something. I open the front door to our Camden flat, Alice still crying her eyes out. I practically carry her into the front room, she's in such a state. I turn the television on as a distraction. It's all over the news. The city we left some 12 hours ago laid to waste. Alice is wrecked by the news, me too. I think about those fashion students. Every one of them will be affected, many will know people who lost their lives in the earthquake. Friends and loved ones. We go downstairs to the basement and climb into bed. We pull the covers over our heads and stay put for a week.

20

I'm your whore

February–April 1995. 1 February, Richie Edwards from the Manic Street Preachers disappears. According to Select *magazine yet another mod revival is imminent. This threat is thwarted in March by a cavalry charge from the old guard, as Cher, Chrissie Hynde, Neneh Cherry and Eric Clapton combine forces for the UK number-one single 'Love Could Build a Bridge'. Elastica's debut album goes into the chart at number one.*

I've got murder on my mind. How to commit the perfect crime. I've already bagged the loot – Polygram Publishing have just paid me a £75,000 advance without hearing a note of any new material – boy, are they going to regret that – so I'm just killing for kicks. I've been rehearsing the band solidly. Four days a week for the past six weeks. The new songs petrify the rank air in our Camden rehearsal studio. On either side the already stale sounds of the rinky-dink Britpoppers, strumming through their forthcoming summer smashes. But in here, in this practice room, they cannot compete with the body count. Man, there's a rotten stench emanating from my brain. The broken bones, the voices goading and the ghosts ominously floating. The earthquake dead, the nervous breakdowns and the sheer jaw-dropping stupidity of the outside world. Songs about death and murder: infanticide, double suicide, bodies incinerated in the heat of an air crash. Crucifixion, dead babies, hotel bombings. Bodies buried in shallow graves, lying on a bed of mud and wires. Death by asphyxiation, death by drowning and even death by choking. Any mode of death you fancy, sir? I'm sure I have it here. If not I'll make one especially for you. Bespoke. Still, at least the band are sounding tight.

Steve Albini's in town and tomorrow we commence recording what will become the Auteurs' third album and my second masterpiece. The record company have booked us into Abbey Road studio number two, where the Fabs recorded all their fab-gear ditties and their sappy hurt-man ballads about ball-busting chicks. It wasn't my idea to use Abbey Road, and it wasn't Albini's – he'd rather use the shitty studio that we both worked in last year – so it must be the record company's. Let's just lay waste to the notion that big expensive studio, hours and hours of recording time and big-shot record producer add up to make a great album. There is not a single case in the history of recording that backs up this theory. So we have 14 days booked from the end of March through to April and Albini working relatively inexpensively (approx £10,000 excluding flights – he will not, as is his way, take a royalty fee). I let the Abbey Road thing slide; occasionally you've got to give the record company something . . . Besides, they have agreed to us working with Albini, a situation that will surely drag them further away from what they really want: a big hit record.

Steve Albini hails from the Midwest: Missoula, Montana, militia country. He has a tendency to speak his mind. On the eve of the recording session he wants to meet the band and myself in a pool hall. No dice. I'm an Englishman. Pool halls? I'm afraid not.

So we meet in a pub, where I can drink alcohol and the teetotal Yank can teetotal.

Unfortunately we get the schoolmaster lecture: 'Make sure you have new drumheads for the snare and replacement strings. Fresh batteries for effects pedals and spare valves for amplifiers. Ensure that all leads are in good working order and that you have enough plectrums.' On and on it goes. I'm half expecting to be told to bring a change of clothing to the studio.

'We'll start at midday and finish at 10 o'clock in the evening. If a song is not working you can take the day off and write a couple of better ones.'

What the fuck is this guy going on about? *Write a couple of better songs.* Who does the septic think he's talking to? This meeting has been terribly unpromising. I hate to follow an obvious line of thought, but I'm wondering where on earth Missoula, Montana and Walton-on-Thames are going to find (un)common ground. It's too late to go back now; we can only push forward. From tomorrow the caper is on.

Abbey Road Studios are steeped in Fabosity. George Martin drifts around, a phantom, looking like he's about to tell you to take your feet off the sofa, and at the back of studio two, where we are camped out, there is some kind of Beatles archaeological dig/necrophilia going on. Old reel-to-reel tape recorders are realigned and old Beatley masters are restored. 'Diddly diddly dum, twiddly twiddly dee,' go the Fabs in three-part harmony on the other side of the wall.[30]

[30] During 1995 the Beatles' master tapes were being plundered for the *Anthology* albums and film. Should have been the last word in Fab overkill but sadly wasn't. The Ruttles responded with their own *Arkeology*. The real Ruttles that is, not the Manchester ones who still clog up the pop charts from time to time.

'The only thing I had in common with Kurt Cobain,' announces Steve Albini in the studio canteen over lunch, 'is that we both hated mushrooms. Why would anybody eat something that grows on shit?' he asks of nobody in particular. An anonymous orchestra troop into the canteen. They are recording a film soundtrack score in studio number one and are now clocking off for lunch. In two weeks' time I doubt if any of the players will recall the title of the film – if they know anyway – or any of the musical themes they have been recording today. The Cellist looks on enviously.

'I'm your whore.' Albini has a catchphrase, a sly acknowledgement for a man who this year (1995) alone has made over 100 records.

'Can I have a little more vocal in my headphones?' says someone.

'Sure,' says Steve Albini. 'Anything you want. I'm your whore.' And so it comes to pass that after a rocky first couple of days, where the whole ship felt like it was drifting off course, everything we now record is sounding immense. 'Buddha' is my art rock monsterpiece, a Van Der Graf Generator stream of conscience/nonsense about a murder in a Cantonese restaurant, driven along by Rockford's huge granite-slab drums and the Cellist's panzer-leader overdrive Hammond. These two cunts are really coming into their own. The magnetic tape spews forth human misery on an unprecedented scale, but you know what, in the studio we are having a fucking blast. Albini seems to have 'gotten' over his initial boss-man-tell-off trip, and is now a fucking riot, the cipher of all sonic DNA. Where, on the second album, the cellos had to be double- and quadruple-tracked, and then drowned in reverb just to achieve a bit of grace, now they are recorded just the once, and are coming on like the Übermensch astride the goddamn mountains screaming out, 'Do you fucking want some?'

We do two takes of my wife-beater classic, 'Married to a Lazy Lover'.

'Er, how was that?' I enquire of take two.

'Fucking A,' answers Albini from the control room.

Are you out of your mind? I think to myself, painfully aware that I might as well have just played my stricken Telecaster with a bunch of bananas.

'Man, that is fucked up,' affirms the American. And he's right, it is fucked up, and it's great. It stayed on the record. There are only two songs that allude to the current scene, and the best of them is 'Tombstone'.[31] I plug my acoustic guitar into a couple of AC 30s, and whack up a horrible MXR distortion box to full throt. If I stop playing then the acoustic will bleed out, an unharnessable tinnitus-inducing wail. So I just thrash away like a moron and don't let up. It's crude, it ain't big and it certainly is not clever. One take for the band and one for the vocal. I fuck up some of the lyrics and miss out a chorus. If it's an epitaph for my 'peers' then it's all they deserve. Albini is also bemused by all this Britpopping going on outside the studio, in the quaint olde worlde of merrie England. 'Which is the one that looks like Herman's Hermits?' asks the American of the tiresome Blur–Oasis kerfuffle. I don't know the answer to this question, but what I do know is that Montana and Walton-on-Thames have formed an alliance.

'What's the name of your group? Oh, Auteurs, the authors, very good.' *Yeah well, kind of, and it's a better name than your group*. Beatle Paul has just come round for tea and he's holding court in the control room. Steve Albini has caught the eye of the assistant engineer, who has now snuck downstairs to the studio, where he will

[31] Contains first reference to Baader Meinhof, albeit erroneously.

quickly and discreetly put away the lifesize cardboard cut-outs of the Mop Tops, liberated by us from a store cupboard and arranged around our instruments in as compromising a manner as possible for cardboard cut-outs. Well, if you will go around having effigies of yourself.

'It's like when I wrote "Yesterday" . . .' continues Macca apropos of nothing, launching into a well-worn story about scrambled eggs and his well-known hurt-man ballad. Lecture over, Beatle Paul then asks if he could hear anything we've been working on. I like McCartney, he's sweet enough and interested. We've just finished recording 'Unsolved Child Murder' and 'After Murder Park' but I politely decline the ex-Beatle's request. I don't want him to be the first person to hear these songs; they're too good for him.

The only blot on the landscape during our two weeks in Abbey Road has been the Cellist's sudden announcement that he has been asked to tour with rock band Therapy. I've already stopped him playing with some hopeless new indie band called Gene, by paying him the same amount that he would have got – to *not* play on the session. I just cannot have my men playing on other people's records as it makes me look bad. I grumpily prepare for a vocal take, inwardly raging at this treachery.

'Can I have a little less drums and a bit more acoustic guitar in the headphones?' I say to Albini.

'Anything you want. I'm your whore.' *You're not the only bloody one, mate*. I think to myself.

After 13 days the job is done. It's been a sweet blag, but now after all the fun and gallows humour, it's time to trawl through the wreckage that has mounted up over the past two weeks. Bodies under the control desk, bodies in the storeroom, bodies on the studio floor, even a dismembered body inside a drum case, and of course bodies all over the master tape. It's time for the dreaded album playback. We just have to mop up now, wipe away any fingerprints, and get rid of any evidence. Can I escape with my freedom? If you can't do the time then don't do the crime.

David Boyd walks into the studio a tad sheepishly and hands Steve Albini an envelope stuffed full of US dollars. It's a classic bit of stage-managed humiliation by the American. Sure there is a practical advantage to being paid cash, but Steve knows that I will enjoy watching my A & R guy act like a guilty husband caught kerb-crawling. I give DB my best cat-who-got-the-cream look and savour his blushes. I'll enjoy it while I still can; the shoe will be on the other foot when they get a whiff of what I'm about to lay on their minds. Yep, it's album playback time.

Turn down the studio lights, heads down for a black mass. Albini switches on the quarter-inch tape machine that he has lovingly sequenced up, complete with carefully timed gaps between songs. Let it roll, Steve.

God this is good, I think to myself, as I gaze at the A & R man's legs pumping up and down – out of time naturally – with 'Light Aircraft on Fire'. Next-up 'Child Brides' takes it down to the speed of death, which, if you need to know, is precisely 3 mph. Any affirmation of living cells hinted at in the opening track is submerged, and I feel myself drowning in the luxury of the eight-piece string section. Take me to the fucking river. Just as the reaper is about to carry me off, I am revived by 'Landlovers'. My near-lifeless body is dragged onto the riverbank and resuscitated, but I don't get off scot-free. By the end of the song I've lost a few old friends and a limb or two. 'New Brat in Town' and 'Everything You Say Will Destroy You' are a wrecked ghost train carrying my ruined soul to the end of side one – yeah! it's a vinyl record – 'Unsolved Child Murder'. Reportage from the crime scene, blank verse with a Mop Top-style French horn. Unlike the previous two elpees this one certainly won't give the French the horn. 'Married to a Lazy Lover' is still 'Fuckin' A'. 'Buddha', an ancient rumble for whom only God knows, and 'Fear of Flying', a medicated monolith, played pre-science slow – for good measure we slow the tape down a little more. Thirty-eight minutes later it's all over, and the album's title track, 'After Murder Park', draws to a close with the pay-off 'I'll love you until the end.' We sit uncomfortably. Silence for a few awkward moments. *Somebody say something then*. All eyes turn to me.

David Boyd – the record company – loves it. The band love it. Steve Albini loves it, and I am in no doubt that this album is some kind of master/monsterpiece. It's just that when the quarter-inch tape machine whirrs to a standstill and the studio lights go back on, the aftershock of listening to a condensed version of the raddled state of my own mind over the last 12 months means that I can only draw one conclusion: that this album stinks like a fucking corpse.

21

Baroque Jesus Lizard

June–July 1995. A bell rings mournfully and throughout London a familiar cry permeates the air: 'Bring out your dead.' And lo, 12,000 corpses are brought to Mile End stadium, where Blur play a concert. Take That are number one in the singles chart. Again.

It's teatime in Camden Town. I've just pulled up the ragged, filthy carpets in my front room, exposing rotting floorboards with gaps between them big enough to fall through. I gaze down longingly. Perhaps one day the floor will do the decent thing and swallow me up whole. Against the wall I have installed a huge iron-framed upright piano. Adjacent to the joanna is the beautiful old French harmonium that I wrote 'Child Brides' on. The entire ceiling is covered with a Palestinian flag that hangs suspended like a parachute, about to smother anyone lucky enough to be standing below. Christ, I hate this fucking house, but at the moment I've got to sit tight, gather up my possessions and shore up. Bunker mentality. The doorbell rings. I'm not expecting guests. Foolishly, I forget to pretend to be out. Oh Lord.

'Man, your apartment looks like shit. What the fuck have you done?' Says Gene Horowitz, unannounced, uninvited and unexpected.

'I live in a Georgian townhouse, not an apartment, but you're right about it looking like shit. What the fuck are you doing here anyway?'

Gene ignores me, pushing past and gaining entrance. 'Mind if my buddies come in – Come on in, Kirk and pals . . .'

Introductions are made and Gene and his three buddies squeeze up together in an awkward line on my tiny two-person sofa. I go off into the kitchen to make a brew and wonder why on earth three quarters of Metallica, whom I have never met before, are sitting in my tiny ruined front room.

Summer 1995. I'm summoned into Hut Recordings. I'm sure they're going to tell me that they've had a change of heart about the album, but they don't. They still love it; they just don't intend to release it for almost a year. This is the way of major record companies: album is recorded in spring; by the time the label gets its act together we're in summer – universities and colleges all on a break, so touring to promote the record is limited, and as for Europe, forget it, no one releases records in Europe in August, everyone is on 'vacation'. September and October, you must be joking, a lot of heavy traffic in autumn. And by November you're going to be running into the Christmas market – enough said. January's a soft chart, so if you put the record out then and it stiffs, then you're going to look really bad. And it's quite likely that it will stiff, because everybody has had the same idea about January, and now the traffic in January is just as heavy as August, so January isn't a soft chart at all. February is a tough nut to crack – all the acts who held back their albums from Christmas and New Year will be releasing now. So that leaves us with spring. Hut releases *After Murder Park* by the Auteurs on 1 March 1996. Twelve days later on 13 March Thomas Hamilton murders 16 children and one adult at Dunblane Primary School, Dunblane, Scotland. Timing is everything.

I wasn't around during Britpop. It's three years now since those first glowing reviews of the band in the weekly music press. I was there at the conception, but perhaps it was just a drunken fumble, something that's best forgotten. During 1993 and 1994 I just seemed to tour, and then the accident confined me to bed. Now in the summer of 1995 the new wave/mod/English rock revival has grown into a monster. Having just made *After Murder Park* I am *psychically* removed from the whole debacle. I am however, physically and geographically at the epicentre: Camden Town. Christ, I can't even go out and buy a pint of milk without being accosted by some chirpy Britpopper. So I lock the doors and hide, and outside chirp takes on the value of saffron. Even dopey soap stars are churning out novelty mockney singles. I stay at home, twiddle my thumbs and contemplate the long wait until the release of my own record. I am lapped and lapped again by no-marks. It's a feeding frenzy for record companies and managers: more white boys with guitars get signed up than you would care to wave a shitty stick at. It occurs to me that having inadvertently sown the seeds for all this cack, enabling the music industry to make a pretty penny, should I not then be on some sort of executive bonus? That or a heavy fine.

Even hopeless saps *The* Verve are getting in on the act. One day in the Hut office Dave Boyd gives me a preview of the crap new *The* Verve track, 'Bittersweet Symphony'. It's the musical equivalent of a child's colouring-in book: simpleton lyrics about, y'know, life sometimes being good and sometimes being bad, taking the rough with the smooth, etc. It even repeats the word 'mould' in the verse – never a good idea.[32] Dave asks me what I think of the song. I tell him the best thing he can do is drop these schmucks, pronto.

Towards the end of summer I take a break from seething, and drag the band away from whatever fun in the sun they are enjoying and back into the studio. I've got a new track – 'Back with the Killer Again' – actually something of a *Murder Park* offcut that we just couldn't nail at the Albini Abbey Road sessions. We rehearse it up, and soon it's a damning, self-mythologising riposte to the current crock that is the UK scene. Steve Albini is not around so I produce myself. Hut seems happy enough for us to while away the time in RAK Studios in St Johns Wood. By the end of the week we have enough tracks to make an EP. I decide to force the record company's hand and get them to agree to release these new tracks as part of a Christmas EP. We'll embrace the tough Christmas chart.

'We cannot fail,' I tell David Boyd, throwing his old line about 'Lenny Valentino' back at him, 'because this is art.' Surprisingly he agrees, so we will have a record out at the very end of the year of Britpop. On the final day of mixing I decide to walk the two miles or so from my Camden home to RAK Studios. Big mistake. Is that figure in the snorkel jacket who I think it is? I make to cross the road, but it's too late – the fucker has clocked me. Oh Christ, he's getting closer. Keep your head down; maybe it'll pass without incident. No fucking chance. The snorkel jacket bears down on me.

'All right pal,' says Noel, now embracing me like some long

[32] The exception to this golden rule of pop being Lieutenant Pigeon's 1972 seminal mother-and-son-performed smash, 'Mouldy Old Dough'.

lost. 'I didn't get the chance to tell you last time we met . . .' Last time. Oh dear God, the nightmare memories of Sweden and Pete Wolf briefly flood back. 'I didn't get the chance to tell you but you've got some top tunes.'

'Cheers,' I splutter back in a clumsy attempt to reciprocate Noel's matyness. Oh dear, it's so disappointing when one's enemies don't turn out to be complete cunts after all.

The three members of Metallica are looking awfully uncomfortable, all squished up in that tiny sofa. I wonder when they are going to leave, but maybe they can't leave; maybe they're stuck and I will have to call the fire brigade in to dislodge them. It must be years since they have had to endure this kind of discomfort.

Gene Horowitz, improbably sensing an impasse between unfriendly host pariah and multi-platinum-global-conquering-rock-godheads, says the worst thing possible: 'Hey, Jesus, I was telling Kirk about your new album.' Then to Kirk Hammett: 'They got Albini in to produce.'

'Woah,' says Kirk Hammett, poodle-haired lead guitar god, inferring a presumed gravitas that no other word could possibly convey.

'Put it on, man' says Gene. 'You've got to get this stuff out into the world; you can't hide it forever.'

Oh but that is exactly what I want to do, hide it forever. Since finishing the album a month or so ago I have been suffering an acute case of buyer's remorse and haven't listened to the damned thing since the studio playback. So with heavy heart I fish out a cassette of what will become *After Murder Park* and prepare to give it its first public airing. I press PLAY and leave 'em to it. I slope off into the kitchen and contemplate putting cutlery in the washing machine and setting it to spin – anything to drown out the depressing din coming from the front room.

'Woah,' says Kirk Hammett.

'It's like . . . It's like . . .' Gene's struggling to tell me what my new album's like. I am actually genuinely interested, as by now I have no idea. Then a breakthrough, a window of clarity in the fog of Gene Horowitz's mind. 'It's like Baroque Jesus Lizard.' Baroque, it should be stated, is pronounced 'bar-roke'. 'Yeah, that's it,' he continues, pleased with himself. 'Baroque Lizard.'

Britpop is reverberating the length and breadth of the country, and I have just invented something called Baroque Jesus Lizard.

'Woah!' says Kirk Hammett. Correctly summarising my predicament. And with that they're off. The three Metallicas and Gene H. troop out the door. Happy to have witnessed the birth of a new musical movement. Woah indeed.

22

A broken panzer and a plastic parrot

August–October 1995. Britpop Now *is aired on BBC2. Albarn plays TV presenter and gets to introduce Gene, Powder, Marion, et al. to the nation. Blur's 'Country House' is number one in the singles chart.* The Great Escape *by Blur goes to number one in the album chart when it is released in September. Hootie and the Blowfish are number one in the US album chart. Noel Gallagher writes an utterly abysmal song named after a George Harrison album. Shockingly he bothers to record the damn thing. Even more shockingly the great British public can't stop buying it. 'Wonderwall' is fucking everywhere.*

'*Guten Abend*,' I offer hopefully at the frankly terrifying middle-aged woman who stands scowling and lost in the middle of the Shoreditch gallery 'space' like a broken panzer.

'Ah, *Guten Abend*,' says the busted tank, palpably relieved and smiling, revealing that, if not exactly a beauty in her prime, then she was at least once a looker. I am required to keep charming her – in German – but before I can reach the part of my brain that deals in elementary Deutsche we are interrupted. The magazine editor who has brought this awkward meeting about steps in and blabs something – in English – about me working on an album about West German terrorism in the 70s. The Frau's face darkens.

'I am not interested in any of that,' booms the German into the pond of Hoxton nitwits, who mill about showing only mild boredom with the photographic exhibition dedicated to the ageing Huness's uncompromising past – the past that she is not interested in. 'I am only looking for a tall man,' she continues sadly, squinting and peering out into the room. Tall man non-forthcoming, our lady fails to bid us *auf Wiedersehen* and storms off into the night.

Momentarily, I am piqued by her terrific Teutonic rudeness. But what the fuck, her photos may be nothing special – any tool can click the shutter on a camera – but can they turn West Germany into a security surveillance state between 1970 and 1977? No, bro, they cannot. For this lady in need of a tall man is Astrid Proll, one-time getaway driver of the so-called Baader Meinhof gang.[33]

Having completed work on the *Back with the Killer* tracks, I reach a recording impasse. There is nothing left to do. It seems as though the brain-ache Britpop party in the summer of 1995 will never end. Alice heads off on holiday to Spain while I remain in London, where I hook up with the only person I want to work with: Phil Vinall. We'll have a little party of our own.

[33] In the interest of fairness, I should state that in the 2003 BBC documentary *Baader Meinhof – In Love With Terror* Astrid Proll displays a dry sense of humour and a clear self-awareness, in sharp contrast to the fleeting encounter described above.

There's a section at the end of 'Bike', on Pink Floyd's debut album *The Piper at the Gates of Dawn*, where Syd Barrett gleefully tries to impress a girl as he tells her about his 'room full of musical tunes'. Then unleashes a cacophony of squeaking, bleeping, belching, jumping, ticking, tocking, chiming and chiding musical and unmusical devices. Phil Vinall's basement flat in Belsize Park is rather like the end of Syd's marvellous mental nursery rhyme. In the time that Phil and I have spent apart, the producer has amassed a fine collection of loony-tune instruments: plastic keyboards from the 70s, an array of ugly-noise-producing bass synths, a Stevie Wonder-like clavichord, a Vox Univibe reputedly once owned and used by Joe Meek, theremins (in several sizes), a couple of children's plastic pianos, an oversized baby's rattle that when shaken produces a bowels-of-the-earth cavernous rumble, and the Holy Grail: a ghastly plastic parrot that, when you scream into its horrid rubbery beak, screams back at you – a kind of extremely effective yet primitive form of sampling. After the Albini album, my relationship with Vinall has become fractious. Whenever an artist goes on to work with another producer, then the original producer gets a dose of the jilted bride at the altar. Phil does his best to make me feel like the Albini album is some sort of bastard offspring, the result of a sordid adulterous affair I would be wise to disown. The spurned producer wastes no opportunity to snipe. He will only have me back if I tell him every sordid detail. So I do. Eventually PV says it's time to put it all behind us, and says that he will take me back – as long as we can make a self-indulgent sonic terrorism elpee together, of clanging tin cans and honking goat horns. Oh well, if that's what it takes.

Phil knows a good thing when it slaps him round the chops, and I've got a cool song in my back pocket. The free-form clanging experiment will have to wait. So we leave the tin cans at home and set off to the studio, Phil's jalopy stuffed to the gills with vintage keyboards, fuzz pedals and tape echo machines. Out of the 'sonic terrorism' equation, I have elected to keep only the terrorism element, and with my head full of 'Enter the Dragon' by Lee Perry, Funkadelic's 'Maggot Brain', 'Up with the Down-Stroke' by Parliament, KC and the Sunshine Band, David Essex, Hot Chocolate and Carl Douglas – not least Carl Douglas, whose classic 'Kung Fu Fighting' I have studied forensically – we go into the abyss once again. Blur's 'Country House' comes on the radio as we pull up outside my favourite east London recording studio. For reasons too numerous and tediously ridiculous to go into, Phil Vinall hates David Balfe – Blur's record label boss and subject of the aforementioned ditty. They have past form together. At first I'm not too worried that dark thoughts of David Balfe will colour the ever-so-slightly-volatile Mr Vinall's mood. After all, I am about to make world-beating art. I start unloading the guitars into the studio foyer.

'Oi, prick. Don't forget these; you'll be needing them,' says Phill Vinall with a face like thunder, thrusting a goat horn and a plastic parrot into my hands.

Post-studio. Sunday night/Monday morning. The goat horn didn't make it but the parrot did. Some would think this an unpromising start for the Baader Meinhof sessions, which will continue into the first half of the next year. Not I. I light a joint and prepare to listen to a cassette copy of the monitor mix of the weekend's work. I haven't been this excited about anything I've done since the first album.

The unforgiving discipline of the string section swoops above me, playing the exotic harmonies that I have ripped from David Essex's 'Stardust' as the second chorus of 'Baader Meinhof' kicks in, then it's into *that* guitar solo. A Gibson SG plugged into an Electro Harmonix Big Muff pedal, plugged into the microphone input of a Fostex four-tracker, plugged straight into the 16-track desk console. *Now you go make a record, arsehole*. Finally the death-head guitar quits trying to kick a hole through the wall of stupidity, and the whole track lurches into a key-change final verse. Over the years I have learnt that upward modulation is not always the most subtle way of sustaining momentum. But we're talking about 'Baader Meinhof' here. Yep, 'Baader Meinhof', you fucking babies. Do you see, I love this record.

The lyrics create a new role for me. This time I cast myself as a news anchorman in a head spin, spouting straight reportage, in between Tourette's bouts of glib pop-art cut-ups. By the end of the track I am just spitting nonsense over the outro. There are no words left. I rewind the tape and roll another joint. I play the fucker a hundred more times and then reluctantly go to bed. I don't want the day to end. Tomorrow will not be able to compete with today.

Midday Monday. I have summoned Manager Tony for the premiere of this masterpiece. I'm all fingers and thumbs as I excitedly fumble the cassette into the player and crank the volume. After a minute, Manager Tony laughs and snorts derisively. 'It's not very commercial, is it?'

I'm not asking you whether it's commercial; the fucking animals in the back garden could tell me it's not commercial. I'm playing it to you because it is good. I do not seek your opinion. It is not required. I know the artistic value of what I have here. I am simply giving you the opportunity to pay your respects. Breathe some rarefied fucking air.

Having pronounced his verdict, Tony shuffles off, no doubt to a meeting with one of his more 'commercial' charges.

*

Tablas and assorted Indian percussion ping away on the Hut office stereo. An Eddie Grant bass synth belches out an enormously dumb riff, followed by the sound of bricks crashing through a window, before the chorus kicks in:

'Baader Meinhof', 'Baader Meinhof'

'Beautiful' David Boyd. Not my affectionate name for the Hut supremo, this bestowal comes courtesy of my label mates *The* Verve. Hahahaha. How I laugh when I first hear this. They may be brainless wig-out scallies from Wigan, but they're always unintentionally fucking funny. Thing is, as I sit opposite Dave B, his leg shaking and head nodding in approval, I'm thinking that the northern hairies may well be right.

The Battle of Britpop is apparently over and the mainstream has been satiated. Everybody is a loser. What the fuck do I care, as David Boyd sits at his desk digging my two new Baader Meinhof recordings. At this point (autumn '95) most major labels might be slightly concerned that their act who was once aligned with Britpop – which will continue to prompt various record company feeding frenzies well into the late 90s – has probably got more in common with Armenian sheep farming than anaemic sub-Kinksian pub-rocking retreads.

'This is fucking great,' says Boyd.

Manager Tony shifts awkwardly next to me on the leather record company sofa. *Not commercial enough? Well it looks like it's gonna be commercial enough to release on a major label, baby.*

'We'll put it out at Christmas along with the new Auteurs single. Do you wanna make an album out of it? Keep it separate from the Auteurs. Baader Meinhof as a side project?'

Yeah, you know it.

Manager Tony is trying to look as if he has been complicit in this all along. I can almost see the cogs whirring away, wondering what cheeky little advance he could possibly procure for a side project called Baader Meinhof.

For this is why I shall always be grateful to 'Beautiful' David Boyd, who either through baffling stupidity or near-psychic comprehension of intuitive artistic greatness – and I'm certain it's the latter – allows and actively encourages me to do what no other major-label A & R man in the worldwide music industry would do: record a concept album about terrorism (at the height/nadir of Britpop) under the name *Baader Meinhof*. I can't resist chancing my arm when Boyd gets up from his desk.

'Good, that's all settled,' I say, hopping into the presidential chair. 'Now I suggest we get on with the serious business of dropping everyone on the label apart from me and signing Vic Goddard.'

'Cheeky cunt,' says David Boyd. Beautiful.

23

'Congratulations on your first number-one record'

December 1995. Pulp's Different Class *is the number-one album in the UK. Meanwhile, Mike Flowers, an unfunny band leader in a comedy wig, releases a version of the aforementioned 'Wonderwall' as a single. Predictable stampede to Woolworths follows, as the faux easy-listening dross is snapped up by the public. Mike Flowers' monstrosity, however, does not quite make the Christmas number-one spot . . .*

Christmas. The season of Noddy and Roy and the time of my re-entry into showbiz. The Britpop hordes have clearly missed me, as have the press and the media, who, tiring of the current mindlessly cheerful pantomime, have taken the new Auteurs single 'Unsolved Child Murder' to their hearts. Ah, you guys. I know the damn thing's got a French horn on it, and it's the festive season an' all, but gentleman, your love for me and my modest art is smothering me. Room to breathe, please, I beg of you.

I know I've hit pay dirt when we make the Radio 1 B-list with ease. Two weeks later and the song is a fixture on the A-list, receiving in excess of 50 plays a week, all over the nation's favourite. The promo schedule is relentless: I'm everywhere, like a madwoman's shit. The radio plugger calls up to tell me I should keep the week before Christmas free, just in case we are asked to perform on the Christmas *Top of the Pops* special. While doing some last-minute shopping in Woolworths the sodding thing gets played 11 times. Look out, this baby's gonna be big. Finally on 17 December I get the call from entertainment central. The Head of Light Entertainment himself comes on the line: 'Congratulations on your first number-one record, and the Christmas number one at that.'

For the rest of the day the phone just won't stop ringing with festive well-wishers and previous holders of the Honour of the Christmas Number One. Late in the afternoon my electronic doorbell chimes out the opening bars of 'Once in Royal David's City': a delivery. The postman hands me a parcel and congratulates me. I tear off the sleigh-bell wrapping paper to reveal a hatbox. I blow away a layer of dust on the lid and find 'Merry Xmas Everybody' written in glitter and stars. I open the box, and with trembling fingers lift out a well worn yet still beautiful top hat covered in mirrors. Inside the hat is a note:

> Congratulations on your Christmas number one
> Here's my crown
> I'm handing it over to you
> Wear it well
> Love
> Noddy

There has been a bit of myth making going on. It is often stated that I released 'Unsolved Child Murder' as a Christmas single.

Wrong. Firstly, 'Unsolved Child Murder' is never released as the stand-alone A-side of a single. In fact it is the second track on the *Back with the Killer* EP. Secondly, this is not released in December 1995, but in January 1996, along with the eponymous 'Baader Meinhof' single. I freely admit to doing nothing until now to contradict this myth. The *Back with the Killer* EP is well received, gaining single of the week in *Melody Maker* and various monthly magazines. John Peel, who previously had not 'enjoyed' the Auteurs, changes his opinion, giving 'Unsolved Child Murder' a few spins. Few others do. 'Baader Meinhof' is another story. While reviewing the *Back with the Killer* EP favourably and running a two-page interview with me, the *NME* chooses to ignore my fabulous terrorist ditty entirely.

Just prior to the release of the BM single, the whole 'concept' has yet to fully crystallise in my mind. So, instead of sending out a press release to hungry journalists, as is standard practice, comprising release date, biography and some bullshit about how the-record-you-are-about-to-play-will-profoundly-change-the-way-you-live-your-life, I up the ante. I photocopy a page from the *Anarchist Cookbook* – a crude American insurrectionary DIY manual from the early 70s – detailing how to construct a nail bomb. That, my friends, is a press release. No further information. On receiving this package, the little boys at the *NME* proclaim the whole stunt 'immoral' and refuse to have anything to do with it. Perversely, Radio 1 gives the 'Baader Meinhof' single a bit of airplay – until they realise what it is about. Strangely, ultra-conservative industry bible *Music Week* proclaim the stunt the 'PR campaign of the year'. Like the great Bloomsbury group hating Vorticist Wyndham Lewis, I am gaining a reputation as something of a contrarian.

The Auteurs' *Back with the Killer* EP peaks at number 48 in the national charts in the second week of January 1996. Most press attention is focused on the second track, 'Unsolved Child Murder', which is generally misunderstood and seen as a grim piece of sensationalist mischief-making. Business as usual. The real Christmas number one of 1995 is 'Earth Song' by Michael Jackson.

24

Piss-poor attitude (TV transgressions part one)

January 1996. On the 15th stalker Robert Hoskins is found guilty of assault and threatening to murder Madonna. Robson and Jerome are number one in the UK album chart, and George Michael is number one in the singles chart with 'Jesus to a Child'.

'Well done, lads,' squeaks the tall man with the thick upstanding shock of red hair in a perfectly irritating Midlands brogue, the highly strung bark of one hour ago now reduced by several levels to a tone that might be described as 'pally'.

I hate you.

'We'll have to get you back when we do it for real,' continues the voice. The voice of stupidity. The voice on the radio. The man on TV.

I don't want to do it for real, I've just done it for real. I certainly don't want to come back, because I never want to see you again. The only thing I want right now is for the lifeblood to drain out of you, and to know that by morning you will be a cold corpse.

'Can I get you a drink?' asks Chris Evans. The subject of my inner – and soon to be outer – rancour, still very much alive and kicking. Evans is an unpleasant creature: a shallow bullying man-child, a jumped-up kissogram-turned-light-entertainment-colossus. Camp commandant of the joyless Radio 1 breakfast show, and now about to extend his métier as a kind of Britpop Joseph Goebbels to a torturous television show of his own creation: *TFI Friday*. Thank fuck it's Friday. I know. Evans and his pet monkeys are the types who think that TV and radio are, you know, like, really, really important, and talk about making 'great TV' and 'great radio' as if they are actually making great TV and great radio. For those who sense an opportunity to get on in life, for those who want to knuckle under or for those who are simply masochists, then Evans is yer man. In the kingdom of the blind the four-eyed man is king. And this dick likes to wield his dick around. The Evans seal of approval is the golden ticket to that mirthless Armageddon they call success. Naturally, radio and TV pluggers will subject themselves to most forms of humiliation just for Evans' producer to tip them the wink. So it is more by bad luck than judgement that the Auteurs, on a miserable day in January 1996, are appearing on the pilot (oh yes, the pilot) for this new *TFI Friday* show, in the hope of one day coming back to perform our new single 'Light Aircraft on Fire'.

'Drink?' repeats Chris Evans.

It's all gone better than I could have hoped. Over at Radio 1 someone has lost their mind. With the previous two releases, *Back with the Killer* and 'Baader Meinhof', It was starting to seem like the only way I was going to get back on the radio was if someone played the records by accident. Now the unthinkable has happened: 'Light Aircraft on Fire' has been added – early doors – to the

Radio 1 C-list. This guarantees it a modicum of daytime airplay (not bad for a song about burning to death at 10,000 feet) and the possibility that it might be promoted to the B-list, giving it wall-to-wall airtime. Even I find myself becoming convinced of the song's, er, crossover potential when I hear a DJ called Nicky Campbell play the track on his afternoon show. As the wall of guitars homes in on the final riff and the song ends, the DJ punches the air with a manly 'Yeeesss' of approval.

Third albums can often spell tricky times ahead, but initially for *After Murder Park* the signs are good. *Select* and *Q* give the record substantial and rave reviews well ahead of release. The sniffy *NME* proves to be positively unsniffy, giving the album eight out of ten and a full-page write-up, noting how this record might not have much and yet everything to do with Britpop. Ah, thank you, ladies and gentlemen. You get the sharpest writing in the *NME*. Only *Melody Maker* misses the point, aiming for a below-the-belt aside: 'New Elvis Costello? More like the new Nick Lowe.'

Unlucky, for even though it ain't true, the journalist makes my day; I love Basher and for me there is no higher honour. Meanwhile, as I juggle with C-lists and half-page slag-offs in the *Melody Maker*, Jarvis, my fellow prisoner in the Fire Records Gulag, is gearing up for his moment of white-heat infamy. Last year's 'Common People' has provided the catalyst, launching Pulp into the abyss that is the hearts and minds of the people: real fame – playing Wembley Arena with Lawrence's Denim in support. Hahahaha. Jarvis, when you become successful leave your friends behind. 'Common People' is a fine record, probably one of the best of the era (though not in the class of, say, 'Kung Fu Fighting').

Unfortunately, this rather good song, and the gentle Michael Jackson baiting, have a depressingly unifying effect on the great British public. Oh God, they've found a spokesman. Do remind me why they have to have a spokesperson one more time? I am (a) Cnut, railing against the crashing tide.

John Peel is on board, say the radio pluggers. 'On board what,' say I, 'the sinking ship?' Nobody laughs. People don't like to be told their accomplishments are a waste of time. So we record a Peel session – my first and last – with Steve Albini on hand to engineer. It's a classic. I pull 'Kid's Issue' out of the air ten minutes before showtime, and we capture it in two takes.[34] It's a startling two-minute chunk of creepy rural malevolence wherein vigilante mobs scour the countryside and backward yokels torture their own.

Steve Albini, pop ears to a man, says it sounds like the Monkees. It doesn't, but that's still high praise. The highlight of the day is when the BBC engineer, who has no idea who Albini is – thinking he is just our pal invited along to give a second opinion – commends the American on his technical proficiency, asking if he has ever thought about a career in the recording industry.

The record company know they have a bad-attitude record to flog and it won't be easy. To their credit, they think it's a record worth persevering with. Though I suspect 'they' really means David Boyd alone, who by now wields enough power to make things happen at will. For my part, I know that to stand a hope in hell of getting my next (almost completed) masterwork released, I will have to bite the bullet and try, really try, to adopt a good attitude

[34] When the Peel Session is released as an EP in mid-'96, as a matter of BBC protocol we are only able to give Steve Albini a 'Thank you' credit due to the session being recorded at the BBC Maida Vale studios with a BBC engineer present and contributing to technical requirements. The credit really should have been: 'Recorded by Steve Albini'.

towards promoting my bad-attitude records. Trouble is, the Auteurs have never been terribly adept at appearing on the box.

Piss-poor flashback. Early 1994. The full band is recording some B-sides for the forthcoming *Now I'm a Cowboy* album. Previously I have been arguing with Manager Tony about a television programme we have been booked to appear on, the long-forgotten *Raw Soup*. It's as good as it sounds. Thick presenters shouting and mugging at the camera as they introduce thick bands and then interact with thick audience members. Of course I will not associate myself with this dreck, and refuse point blank to turn up. Manager Tony, as ever, is infuriated. I have already turned down *The Word*, an entirely execrable show. Tony will have to make his excuses to the increasingly impatient record company. He'll think of something; he's a fantasist. He has to be – he manages the Auteurs.

The studio phone rings, it's David Boyd for me.

'Hi, how're you doing?' says Dave on the other end.

I'm brusque, irritated at being interrupted when I'm working. 'I'm fine. What can I do for you?' I manage.

'You all right?' questions Boyd, his voice quiet and concerned. 'I'm surprised you're working . . .'

Something's up.

'Why wouldn't I be?'

'The accident?' says David, both of us now confused and suspicious. 'The accident and Barney,' clarifies DB.

'Look, there's been no accident,' I say, looking over at Barney C. Rockford, accident-free drummer, who is sitting at his stool bemused that he is now the unwitting star of a conspiracy.

'You mean there was no crash?'

'Not as far as I know.' The penny starts to drop.

'Ah,' concludes David. 'Your manager Tony Beard phoned me last night to say Barney's family had been killed in a helicopter accident in South Africa, and you wouldn't be able to do that TV show.'

'Let me just check,' I offer. 'Nope, Barney's fine.' I glance over at the non-grieving drummer convulsing with laughter. 'In fact he's very well. Maybe Tony should have remembered to tell me,' I add, slightly disappointed at his carelessness, but full of admiration for the audacity of my manager's preposterous fib. 'The lying little cunt,' says Boyd, half amused, half livid, before signing off. Some people will go to extraordinary lengths to appear on television, and some people will go to even greater lengths to avoid appearing on it.

The *TFI Friday* pilot has been put to bed, and now we can relax in the bar on board the ship of fools. It's been a relentlessly nasty little day. The kind of day where you would willingly lose a few limbs or indeed your own life, if only the IRA would bomb this TV studio in Hammersmith. Television exists in a time of its own: seconds become minutes, minutes become hours and days become weeks. For every hour that passes the clocks seem to go back another two. We have now spent twelve mind-numbingly horrendous hours in the company of these dummies from the telly, and we have recorded a no-doubt-awful one-hour dummy – for the telly. Throughout the twelve hours Evans has been monstrous. Yelling at assistants about nothing, behaving like a fucking moron, screaming like a toddler as he throws himself on the floor in tantrums. I long for one of his lackeys to snap and lamp the obnoxious bully, but of course they don't because they all know that if they were to step inside his shoes, they would behave exactly the same way. That is how you get on in television. At one point he bawls out the entire studio, catching himself as he makes it clear that he does not include 'the bands' in this tirade. The pussy.

Ah, the bands: we are to share the floor with a revived Ocean Colour Scene, Brit R & B no-hopers from the Midlands. Evans has predictably taken a shine to these dunces. Having been informed that Britpop is all the rage, the DJ has taken a firm hold of the wrong end of the shitty stick. I order a drink at the bar and hope that my cab arrives soon. A member of Ocean Colour Scene drunkenly skids past me on his knees and draws blood. He looks down at his bloodied knee and then up at me. Like a little boy, hurt and embarrassed at being caught out. For a moment I think I see a tear in his eye.

Then he speaks: 'I'd fookin' loik to give 'er one, wouldn't yow?' The idiot on the floor makes a gesture toward the ex-soap actress preening on the sofa, twittering on about her bright future in Hollywood.

'No, I really wouldn't,' I say. Leaving the Brummie confused and still on the deck.

Our television plugger fusses around the show's producers, desperately trying to get a bit of 'feedback'. Eventually Manager Tony sidles up to me at the bar. 'The producer really liked the performance today, and they really like 'Tombstone' from the album. If we put that out as a single, then they'll have us on the show,' whispers Tony, barely able to contain his excitement.

Jesus, I only did this because I want to make sure that the record company put out my beautiful low-concept album about terrorism. Now you're going to let this fucking coxcomb dictate to you?

Danny Baker – one of the masterminds behind this TV atrocity – walks by with a bun in each hand. He crams one of the buns into his mouth.

Evans beckons again. 'Drink?'

It's a do-or-die situation. I take the latter option. I look him in the eye across the bar and slowly and deliberately mouth two words at him: 'Fuck. You.' And then: 'Cunt.' It's an afterthought, and it registers. He half smiles and walks out of my eye line. He knows.

My car has arrived. The pluggers and Manager Tony bundle themselves into cabs, oblivious to my heroic intervention, greedily totting up the value of a bit of Evans approval. Some people will go to extraordinary lengths to get themselves off television.

25

Let's get the fuck out of Hertfordshire (TV transgressions part two)

February 1996. Babylon Zoo are number one in the UK singles chart with 'Spaceman'. 'Don't Look Back in Anger', Oasis' brainless oafish anthem about nothing at all, lumbers into the number-one spot, where it remains for one week. It feels a lot longer.

Someone hasn't learnt their lesson. We are about to do a run-through for the cameras. I am wearing the National Health-style bins I bought in Japan, the glasses that I do not need, that I am now attached to and that are attached to me. The glasses that protect me from the outside world. The glasses that will hide *me* from *you*, inside *your* television set. Derek Hood, the stand-in for my crocked drummer, sitting behind me at his drum kit, has gamely agreed to don the IRA balaclava I have provided. Del has not so gamely demurred at wearing the home-made *Direct Action Against Drugs* T-shirt I have also kindly provided him with.[35]

[35] Direct Action Against Drugs: a vigilante group that carried out the murder

Quite reasonably arguing that it is a) not funny, b) it might get him killed. To my left Barney C. Rockford sits in a wheelchair, purposefully operating an elaborate remote control unit that rests on his lap. The remote control unit does nothing; when he's not fiddling with its switches and buttons, the out-of-action drummer idly reads a newspaper with the mocked-up headline AUTEURS BREAK UP ON RE-ENTRY.[36] Look Ma, I'm on telly.

There's gold in them there hills. The 'Light Aircraft' gravy train just rolls on and on. We're still on the C-list, but we (the radio and TV pluggers) have hope in our hearts. Lord alone knows why. Today, one week on from the Chris Evans fiasco, we are on the march towards George Harrison's stately home in Hertfordshire. The Quiet One has lent out his country pile to the Natural Law Party, to whom he is giving his backing in the next general election. The NLP are a harmless mob, fin-de-siècle mumbo-jumboists, whose manifesto seems mainly to be concerned with Transcendental Meditation and yogic flying. They are kindly hiring out George's gaff to ITV, who are kindly filming a shit new music show there called *Hotel Babylon*. Hotel. Babylon. Friday night watch-after-the-pub-and-then-kill-yourself TV. George may be backing a loser with the Natural Law Party, but frankly they have more chance of winning an election than *Hotel Babylon* does of getting a second series.

---

of six drug dealers in Northern Ireland. Widely believed to be a front for the Provisional IRA.

[36] This headline relates to a news story that appears in both the weekly music papers, when I drunkenly blurt out to a journalist that I have no intention of making any more Auteurs albums and that an artist should never record more than three albums. Quite a strange statement considering that at the time of the interview, I was close to finishing work on *Baader Meinhof* – my fourth album.

The promotional video for 'Unsolved Child Murder' is just a couple of long shots edited together. A 16-millimetre camera looking out unflinchingly at the country lanes ahead from the car dashboard. Two takes: one by day, one by night with the car headlights providing the only lighting. This is all my own work. My one and only attempt at filming, editing and directing. The record company humour me of course: it's a great film but it ain't gonna sell the song to anyone. How do you sell the unsaleable? Hut Recordings will doubtless attempt to come up with a way. Why don't we make an animated video. Ahahaha. An animation for a song about a missing child. Please let me see the treatment right now. Eventually some sort of sense prevails, and it is decided that we will make a promotional video for the 'Back with the Killer' track instead, using hotshot young film-maker Chris Cunningham. Cunningham's already been involved in the *After Murder Park* sleeve, manipulating the inner photograph so that the children pictured all have a digitally morphed version of my face. It's a winning sleeve. Chris thinks so as well, as he will recycle it again and again in his work with one-man-tidying a-shed electro-yokel Aphex Twin. Cunningham's a clever lad for sure, keen as mustard. He claims that the *New Wave* album got him into guitar bands. Well, it's a sweet thing to say. His storyboard for the promo is however unpalatable and appears to have very little to do with the song. Helpfully, I am refusing to appear in the damn thing, so when the video is eventually shot in a psychiatric hospital outside London we have an emaciated naked man, replacing me, whose last acting job was playing a concentration camp victim. In between lip-syncing the words the apparently starving man vomits on the floor.

February is a busy month. My diary is full of pointless chores and joyless activities. In a record company screening room I have just watched myself turn into a doggy. Alice is a cutesy pink fluffy-wuffy kitten, Barney C. Rockford is Mr Porky Pig, and the Cellist is a lovely wabbit. We are watching a cut of our new video for 'Light Aircraft on Fire' and David Boyd is a little less red-faced with anger than he was a few months ago.

The 'Back with the Killer' video was not a success on any level. I was a naughty boy. I pushed and pushed Chris Cunningham into stepping over the line, and boy did he step over that line. Boyd (and the paymasters at Virgin Records) are appalled. There is a stony silence after a rough cut is previewed, 'What exactly is the point of this video?' asks Boyd thunderously. This is a very difficult question to answer, having just watched someone who looks like an Auschwitz prisoner lip-syncing with only half a face in a padded cell as various SM dwarf ladies suck up their own vomit.

At a later screening a producer from *The Chart Show* walks out, claiming that she too is about to vomit. So, not entirely a failure. Anyhow, Cunningham has gained a bit of notoriety from the whole wayward affair, and has somehow avoided the boot from the record company. In a marvellous display of music-biz logic defiance, he has wound up as director of our new reverse-anthropomorphising 'Light Aircraft on Fire' video.

Me, I don't give a damn. I have grown tired of videos. The 'Showgirl' promo back in '92 was OK, but I have a pretty low boredom threshold; there are plenty of things I would rather do than lip-sync along to a song recorded a year ago. But the 'Light Aircraft' video seems to be going down well with everyone – apart from, I suspect, the director, whose sarcastic morphing of the band into cuddly pets (although I am actually a pit bull) is a subtle riposte to the ticking-off we all received for that last God-awful video. So now we have something that can actually be shown, which is apparently all that matters. All we need to do now is get on that Radio 1 B-list. Oh, and there is the small matter of that *Hotel Babylon* TV show.

The rain beats down on our Portakabin. Inside the Portakabin the producer of *Hotel Babylon* beats down on us. Firstly, he's not very happy about the mocked-up copy of the *Daily Mail* that Barney is brandishing. Secondly he's not very happy about Barney. What we assume to be the problem is that Barney C. Rockford is going to be subverting his usual role as Auteurs drummer for this TV performance by sitting reading the paper in a wheelchair. The rather spurious reason for Rockford being wheelchair-bound is that he has recently broken his shoulder and is unable to drum – hence Del sitting in for him. The producer seems unconcerned that Del is dressed as a member of the Provisional IRA, but he's getting a big old bee in his bonce over Barney.

A rather surreal argument ensues about disabled rights between myself, Barney and the producer. Our TV plugger sits nervously in the corner hoping to be swallowed up by the temporary floor. It must be a soul-destroying job at the best of times, not made any easier when a bunch of idiots wants to subvert some fluffy TV cack by littering the stage with people pretending to be disabled terrorists.

The argument is now picking up pace, with people shouting about hypothetical situations concerning Robert Wyatt and Ian Dury. I try my best to shoehorn in that one-armed drummer from Def Leppard but miss my moment. The argument is only resolved when I stop shouting and realise that the producer is not that bothered about the wheelchair; he is in fact more concerned that Barney does not appear to be using the remote control unit (that does nothing) enough. A compromise is reached, and it is agreed that Barney will make more use of the remote control unit (that does nothing). The producer only has one more bugbear: what to do about that mocked-up copy of the *Daily Mail*.

The studio audience are a motley bunch of provincial clubbers, kerb-crawled in Leicester Square by some desperado researcher with an offer they ought to refuse: the chance to be in the audience for *Hotel Babylon*. Difficult though it is to comprehend, people really have nothing better to do with their Wednesday afternoons and actually accept this offer. The warm-up man works his magic on the indifferent clubbers.

'In a few minutes I'm gonna be introducing a band called the Auteurs. Now, it might not be your sort of thing, but I want you to all look like you're really into it. Go wild, if you can.' Having cast his hypnotic spell, the warm-up man then bounds over to where the band are standing. 'Great, I think they're ready for you,' he says, smiling manically at me. This is as close as this bozo is going to get to a Radio 1 roadshow.

'One thing,' I say before the dimwit rushes off to do his intro. 'It's my birthday, and it would be great if you could get the audience to sing "Happy Birthday" to me.'

Fifty hungover clubbers finish singing the last line of a very unenthusiastic rendition of 'Happy Birthday to You'. The warm-up man stops conducting and showbiz-style shouts, 'Ladies and gennelmen, give it up, *Hotel Babylon-style, for the Auteurs . . .*'

He's got them in a frenzy, creating just enough of a smattering of applause for the real presenter, a blonde woman, to witter something about 'bedsit music' from her podium and 'hand over' to us.

The dwarf's stage invasion in Strasbourg flashes through my mind. I know now what I have to do – what I should have done to that cunt. I lean back, and before he knows it the toe of my boot has connected with the warm-up man's sorry behind, and within a second he's down on the ground . . . and off my fucking stage.

We crash through the song as fast and hard as possible. Rockford furiously pumping away with one hand on his useless remote control button, the other hand brandishing a copy of the mocked up AUTEURS BREAK UP ON RE-ENTRY *Daily Mail* in the direction of the unsmiling producer. The warm-up man has taken being booted off stage rather well. He is now down the front banging his head and spinning around and generally showing the clubbers how to go mental to the beat of something called 'Light Aircraft on Fire'. I look around and notice that our TV plugger has left the building.

We are the Stones at Altamount. We bound offstage after our one-song performance, bypass the dressing room and jump straight into our people carrier. Hit the gas, driver. Let's get the fuck out of Hertfordshire. Leave the Angels to sort out the gear, and the carnage we've left in our wake.

'Light Aircraft on Fire' gets stuck on the Radio 1 C-list for a couple of weeks and finally crashes into the pop charts at number 52. The TV producer goes on to make many more music TV shows, gradually rising up the ranks, and for a time, in the late 90s becomes quite powerful in music television. Our paths do not cross again.

26

When your fuck-up ISA reaches full maturity

March–May 1996. Take That have another number one in the singles chart followed by 'Firestarter' by The Prodigy. In April Mike Leander, producer and co-writer of many of Gary Glitter's 70s hits, dies of cancer. 'Three Lions' by Baddiel, Skinner and the Lightning Seeds is, by May, unavoidable.

'Just do it,' I say to Jerry, our tour manager, in response to his question. Our tour bus is at the bottom of a ditch. A cocktail of human error and exasperation has forced our vehicle off the freeway just outside Washington DC en route to New York City.

'Shall I just drive the fucker into that crash barrier?' asks Jerry, quite reasonably for a man who has lost all sense of reason. I'm riding shotgun and the Cellist is in the back with his head in his hands.

'Yeah, just do it,' I urge. Jerry and I have intuitively arrived at the same conclusion: that so far on this cursed tour every damn move we make turns to shit. The logical thing to do now is pre-empt. Cut out the middleman. Go for broke. We accept that the

Fates have got it in for us, so if they are watching from above we will make them this offering. Then please leave us alone. Jerry takes off the handbrake, puts his foot down and rams the bus into the crash barrier, with a satisfying crunch. It's the most fun we've had so far on this nightmare tour. As far as sacrifices go though, it's not enough.

One more roll of the dice then. Lucky, lucky USA. The Auteurs – or should that be I? – now have an American manager (as well as an English one). The American manager has been brought in 'to take care of business stateside'. This would imply that my career is skyrocketing across the Atlantic. This is not the case, and the notion that anybody needs to 'take care of business stateside' is both vain and delusional. However, the music industry runs on blind optimism, and the American manager is doing his job. Having noticed that in the United States, no one gives a hoot about all these pansy Britpoppers, he has also sussed that *After Murder Park* ain't no pansy Britpop album. The American manager and our New York booking agent Marty Diamond have put their heads together and concluded that a short pre-(US)-album-release acoustic tour will be just the ticket, and will enthuse all those American fans who came along to the sold-out *Now I'm a Cowboy* tour two years ago. The American manager and Marty D are both wrong.

'It's great and everything, but is anyone really going to buy it?' The Drummer has just served me a critical open sandwich, several weeks before the release of *After Murder Park*. On 1 March Barney C. Rockford will have his answer. No. *After Murder Park* goes into the album chart at number 33, drops to 52 then buggers off. Some 58,000 copies are sold, in a staggered worldwide release, over the next six months. Six years ago this would be no mean feat, as most

British and American so-called guitar bands struggled to net sales of 10,000. But, post-Nirvana and lost in the Britpop pea-souper, the album's initial sales in the UK are seen as disappointing. To whom? Well, not to David Boyd, not to me – I expected no more and no less – and not to Mr B. C. Rockford. A few weeks after the record's release I decide to make good on my drunken threats in the music press. On a dreary Monday evening in the middle of March 1996 Alice and I meet Barney and the Cellist in a dismal restaurant near Waterloo Station. We have a dreary 'night out' and I tell everyone that after touring commitments have been fulfilled there will be no more Auteurs.

'Yeah, that seems like the right thing to do,' says Rockford. I scrutinise his face for evidence of sarcasm; after all, I am effectively giving him his P45. Nope. The drummer is just continuing his metamorphosis into the archangel of truth. I'm actually pretty happy about the whole thing. The lack of sales, which I had expected, is not the primary motive – it's just a reason to give people for cutting off their money. The real reason is that I can't see much further into the future than my beloved *Baader Meinhof* album, scheduled to be released in seven months' time (November '96). *Baader Meinhof* is effectively a solo album. Since the recording of *After Murder Park* with Albini, the Auteurs have got used to recording live, as a group. Now, after *Baader Meinhof*, I have once again found the chops to be a solo artist, just as I did when I was writing and recording the demos for *New Wave*. So, the Auteurs' greatness as the *real* group who recorded *After Murder Park* will be their undoing. Whatever the future holds for me, the Cellist and Rockford ain't in it. Alice, I know, is miserable – she feels like she's given this band her all over the last four years, and for what? Sweet nothing, and she's absolutely right. She will never really forgive me. I don't blame her. The Cellist's reaction is the most surprising: he is visibly shocked, didn't see it coming at all. At first I think that he's just going to miss his wage, but as the depressing evening drags on I hear his voice falter. Fuck, he really does care.

Touring commitments. Oh yes, this is the reason I started writing songs, making records. There is a British tour and a European tour scheduled for later in the year, but right now, in April 1996, Jerry the tour manager, the Cellist and I are trapped in New York, attempting to fulfil touring commitments a few weeks prior to the US release of *After Murder Park*.

The Cellist and I have had a couple of rehearsals – this is a money-saving two-hander – him on electric cello, glockenspiel and anything else he can bang or pluck whenever he has a free moment.

I start getting a mild sense of foreboding when he takes me aside to warn me of his vision of the future: 'This tour is going to be very strange, you do know that?' I can see the panic in his eyes.

Comedy New Yorker Marty Diamond hasn't changed: he still imagines his life as one long Scorcese movie. Between comedy banter with the owner of the East Village coffee shop – Sal or Vinnie, no doubt – he is cheerfully telling me that most of the US tour is now cancelled. Poor ticket sales. It's a shame that neither Marty nor the American manager bothered to check the advance sales before we got on the plane. I feel my temper rising.

'Don't worry about it,' assures Marty. 'It just means that you get more time to hang out in New York, then you can do the Boston and DC gigs' – which unfortunately remain on the schedule.

'At least you get to go home early – back to all those English groups,' adds the American manager snidely, before gleefully reeling off a list of crap Britpop bands. I should smash these two goons' heads together, but the will to fight back has deserted me.

Then Marty lands the killer blow: 'You know, it's all rock 'n' roll.'

'Except it's not, Marty . . .' is all I can weakly counter with before my knees buckle under me.

For three days and nights I rattle around in the Gramercy Park Hotel. I get drunk with some English girls in the bar, but I mainly feel like a fool. NYC is no fun when you've had the stuffing knocked out of you. The Cellist has not been seen for days. Never mind, we are soon to play in Boston, where Marty Diamond has assured me that he has not booked us to play a sports bar.

I look at the baseball flags on the wall then at the Cellist. Defeat in his eyes. Same as me. There are no posters advertising our presence, there is no real PA and there is no promoter, just a barrage of sports commentary from the TV high above the bar and a handful of Boston Redsox fans who exchange sporting banter at one another as they sip their Buds and wonder why the fuck these English people are sat in their bar, and what the fuck are they planning to do with that guitar and that other thing. I don't intend to let them find out.

Jerry comes back into the bar. He has been scouting around, and yes, we are booked to play in this dive.

'Do you want to call Marty? says the Cellist wearily.

'Not really,' I say. 'Let's just go.' So we go. Off map, electing not to stay at our prebooked hotel in Boston. Why stick to the plan when so far it has not served us well? Off we drive to nowhere in particular, yet to play a date on our final American tour.

There is a good chance that we may play tonight, en route to Washington DC from Mystic. Mystic, where we stayed the previous night in a cheap motel, and where the only place open to eat is a bar and grill joint. The staff refuse to serve me drink unless I provide them with ID. I cannot be bothered to find my passport so I sit in front of a huge plate of food. Stone cold sober, watching the daddy of a little girl on the table in front of us making lascivious comments to his little princess. I go back to my motel room and I want to die.

Can we retain one shred of dignity from this unfolding disaster? One thing that might make it all worthwhile is the 9.30 Club, Washington. We've played here many times, but the place has been revamped. The rats the size of cats have deserted the venue. They're not the only ones to have fled. Most of our audience has gone AWOL as well. But we cannot cop out, so the Cellist and I put on a fine show for the hundred or so people who show up. Our one and only show on this stricken American tour.

I get the knock on my hotel room door at 5.30 a.m. The Cellist. He's been up all night on the blower to Blighty. He can't take it any more and is trying to book himself on the first flight back. Normally I'd go fucking ballistic, but I know he's not a quitter so he must be in a bad way. He is. Finally, we manage to book him on a flight leaving New York on Sunday. Three days away. We all arrange to meet downstairs in an hour, the plan being to safely drive back to NYC. The Cellist is excelling himself: not content with wrecking what remains of the tour, he has now, somehow, managed to lock us out of our van. I'm liking the Cellist more and more. It's the first time he's fucked up in four years. It's like he's got all this credit in the fuck-up bank and it's now paying out as one enormous fuck-up dividend. We loiter uncomfortably on the sidewalk for an age waiting for a locksmith and batting off the junkies and crackheads who offer to help look after our bags. After several hours we are able to commence our journey, crash the tour bus – almost as soon as we are out of Washington – and slowly limp back to New York, where we have nothing to do but wait for our flight. Can we retain one shred of dignity from this unfolding disaster? Not likely.

In the bar of an NYC Holiday Inn the American manager is mulling over our recent travails. He doesn't want me to play Monday's show at the Mercury Lounge solo. Of course it's the wrong decision – he's been wrong all the way down the line – but I don't bother arguing with him. There is nothing here to salvage. Then the American manager gives me his funny line once again: 'Just think, you get to go home early, back to England and all those English bands.' And he's off with his hilarious list of crap Britpoppers: 'The Bluetones, Shed Seven, Oasis, Echobelly, Northern Uproar . . .'

The Cellist is suffering badly – won't, no, *can't* leave his room at the Holiday Inn until we're due to leave for the airport. Jerry's deliberate crashing of the van may have pushed him over the brink. His fuck-up ISA has now fully matured, serious stuff for such a bourgeois culture fiend stranded in New York City. I try talking him down, but he's got to work this one out for himself. I really have been caught off guard at how the break-up of the group has affected him. I thought he didn't give a damn when he actually really cares. Did he care right from the beginning? I don't know. But I do know that I have misjudged him. Sunday comes round and the three of us make our bedraggled journey to JFK. It's one of the few times I board an aircraft with a sense of relief. America is no longer the land of possibilities. It is the land of impossibility, a land where a previously mentally robust cello player has temporarily lost his mind, forcing us to come home early – from a tour that was mainly cancelled – having played one show to a smattering of people. I am also in receipt of a huge repair bill for the hired tour bus that Jerry (with my blessing) deliberately crashed. This whole shambles is rammed home when I open up the copy of *Details* magazine I have bought to read on the plane. There in the music section is the lead review, a whole page dedicated to *After Murder Park*. Ditto *Rolling Stone*. When we were actually *in* the States there were no interviews scheduled. As soon as I am home, the US interview requests start coming in thick and fast. The Auteurs: once again ahead of their time.

27

Baader Meinhof revue

July–November 1996. Fugees are number one in the singles chart with 'Killing Me Softly'. In August the Ramones play their last show. Robson and Jerome clog up the November charts.

Through the kaleidoscope of shit that is 1996 – the undignified TV appearances, the unexciting record sales, the unstoppable rise of my inferiors, the end of my group and the rotten corpse that I have to drag one more time around the live circuit[37] – I remain true to my one obsession: completing the recording of the *Baader Meinhof* album and doing as little as possible to fuck up its release. The sessions become almost covert as I am supposed to be putting all my efforts into promoting *After Murder Park*. Everyone involved in the recording is sworn to secrecy. Like Vorticist Wyndham Lewis in the 20s, when he was writing for *The Enemy*, I do my best to stir up a false sense of paranoia.

[37] During the summer of 1996 the Auteurs continue to fulfil commitments with short British and European tours. Both are workmanlike and subdued.

Good for a record like this. So why did I make a concept album about terrorism?

There's no way round it, the iconography and language of the urban guerrilla is far superior to the iconography and language of rock. Patti Smith knew this when she first clapped her eyes on the other Patty: Hearst, the heiress kidnapped by the Symbionese Liberation Army in 1974. Of course, the SLA were one of the most deluded, incompetent terror cells to have ever existed. When Smith turned the old blues garage standard 'Hey Joe'[38] into an incantation about Hearst, she wasn't to know this. What she did know was that Hearst, posing with an AK-47 in front of the ridiculous seven-headed SLA flag, looked cooler than all those bag-of-bones English rockers she'd loved from afar, growing up in New Jersey. Immortal rock deities just cannot compete with terrorist chic, 70s style: Jimmy Page in German officer cap going down on his twin-neck SG with violin bow; Iggy smeared in peanut butter, walking on the crowd in Cincinatti in 1970, or covered in his own blood at Rodney's English Disco four years later; the Pistols, jubilee boat trip; The Clash as urban guerrillas in, er, Camden Town. Fuck that. Show me the grainy footage of the Baader Meinhof gang undergoing basic training with the PLO in Jordan; the capture of Andreas Baader, with long bleached hair and Ray-Bans; a propaganda photograph of Leila Khaled, the beautiful Palestinian plane hijacker, posing with Kalashnikov in 1970. I'll even take one fat boy over another. You can keep your front cover of *Absolutely Live* – Jim Morrison in leathers. I'll take that one grainy mugshot of dough-faced Carlos the Jackal any day. Immortality or inhumanity. Rock 'n' roll can only supply a secular version of the former, while terrorism provides a clear

[38] The 1974 B-side of Smith's first single: 'Piss Factory'.

path to both. The *Baader Meinhof* album: a record that is just begging to be judged by its cover. Terrorist chic; you've gotta love it.

Halfway through the making of the album I meet an old friend – an old-school Glaswegian anarchist (old-school in the sense that in his younger days he would think nothing of piling into a van with a few other like-minded souls, roaring down the motorway to some demonstration or other and chucking a few petrol bombs into the mix). After five or six hours' heavy drinking the friend and I end up in an illegal Soho gambling club. As the drinks take their toll, starts getting more and more agitated about the terrorist-themed album I am about to unleash. Finally, having been asked to leave the premises, he pins me against a wall and spits in my face, 'You've got no right to be making a record like this, unless you can point a gun at women and children and be prepared to use it.'

Of course I can't. And maybe he's right, but he's missing the point: this is a *record* about terrorism, nothing more.

Heads will roll. That was my promise to David Boyd's office answer-phone, as I cut loose with the invective, trying not to crack up, hermetically sealed inside the Holiday Inn at the end of *that* American 'tour'. I didn't lose my mind in New York; I saved all that until I got home.

The meeting takes place in the ever-yo-yoing Hut office. David Boyd, Alice, Manager Tony Beard and I. The first thing to do is yell at Manager Tony, which I do for several minutes, although to everyone else present it must feel like several excruciating hours. Then it's time to make a call. I tell Tony to phone Comedy Marty Diamond right now and fire him in front of everyone.

After all, it was Marty who booked the tour way in advance of any press, and way in advance of the album coming out, in even more inappropriate venues than usual, and who either didn't notice the poor advance ticket sales or just didn't bother telling anyone before we flew out to the States.

Manager Tony coughs and splutters, finally speaks to Marty . . . and in the most spineless, obsequious, apologetic way, clears his throat one last time and fires the agent. Tony manages several other bands that Marty represents, and before the phone call is over tactless Tony has managed to tie up a few other bits of business. Comedy Marty and Comedy Tony bid each other fond adieus until next time. Big fucking mistake. David Boyd winces; he sees it coming.

The following day I waste no time sacking Manager Tony with as few words as possible. He's lucky, I saved him the indignity of being given the boot in front of an audience. If the map is of no use any more, you might as well drive the wagon off the road. With my work cut out, it's clear I don't need a manager, although when I alert my minions – agent, publisher, PR and plugger – that I am now the main man they must deal with, there is a mass migration to the hills.

Come back, guys, it's just lil ol me, and soon I'll have a shiny new concept album about terrorism in the 70s for you all to work on. Don't be a stranger now.

Obviously, there is a gathering army of detractors among the suits at Virgin who would like to pull me out of my safe house at Hut and make me walk the plank. I'm not that bothered. As far as I am concerned, while I am still signed, they all work for me. A bit of dissension from the shit shovellers is not always such a bad thing – let the workers blow off a little steam. Besides, I still have my man at the top.

David Boyd and I are in agreement: *Baader Meinhof* is a masterpiece of both artistic intent and production. Dave's getting worried though. He fishes out a fax from on high that concludes with the statement: 'I would like to remind you that Virgin Records did not sign Luke Haines to make political statements. He is signed as an entertainer.'

'Hahahahaha. My God, this is faaaabulous,' I crow.

DB is not quite as amused. He's getting grief from top brass.

'Do you think the Manics have ever had a fax this good? Did CBS ever say this to The Clash? Well, if they want entertainment, then entertainment is what I shall give them. Can you fly me to Munich? With a photographer?' I ask. The following weekend I am whisked off to the Bavarian capital for a photo shoot at the Munich Olympic Stadium, where in 1972 13 Israeli athletes were shot dead in a Black September attack.

The real Baader Meinhof gang rose from the ruins of the counterculture, and for ten years turned West Germany into a high-security surveillance state. 1967. The Summer of Hate. Twenty years since the Nuremberg trials. In West Berlin student demonstrator Benno Ohnsborg is shot dead by police. At a rally soon after political activist Gudrun Ennslin gives a good speech: 'Violence is the only way to answer violence. This is the Auschwitz generation and there's no arguing with them.' Gudrun soon comes into the orbit of Andreas Baader, a pathological car thief and a fucking hooligan with no interest in revolutionary politics whatsoever. He is, however, quite keen on blowing stuff up. Baader and Ensslin's first act of situationist-inspired mayhem begins in the radical spring of 1968, when they firebomb two Frankfurt department stores. They are sentenced to three years' jail in mid-'69, but go on the run instead, opting to become full-time urban guerrillas, until

Baader's eventual re-arrest six months later for reckless driving in a stolen Mercedes.

Andreas Baader's final escape from prison in May 1970 is the catalyst for the future of West German terrorism. Baader is working in the prison library when an armed girl gang, including well-known journalist Ulrike Meinhof – a kind of (young) Julie Burchill of her day – burst into the building in a hail of Beretta bullets and tear gas. Baader jumps out of the window and into an Alpha Romeo – at the wheel of which is fast driver Astrid Proll. The Alpha is later dumped and recovered; a copy of *Introduction to Das Kapital* is found under the driver's seat.

The group now become known to the press and the public as the Baader Meinhof gang. For two years mayhem ensues. Firstly Baader, Ensslin and Meinhof fly to Damascus to undertake armed training with the PLO. Ulrike Meinhof decides that her two children should be brought up in a Palestinian orphan camp. It's the correct revolutionary thing to do, you see. By 1971 the group are going under the name of the Red Army Faction and gaining members all the time, in particular a bunch of very far out psychiatric patients who call themselves the Socialist Patients Collective (SPK). Boy, this lot are gonna be hard work. Soon the SPK – mental patients on the run – and the RAF are unleashing a trail of chaos, destruction and death throughout West Germany.

In mid-'72 Baader is arrested following a two-hour shoot-out broadcast live on West German television. Soon after, Gudrun Ensslin – in black-face disguise – is arrested in a department store. Ulrike is shopped by a sympathiser who donates the reward money to the RAF defence fund. Baader, Meinhof and Ensslin, after a lengthy and chaotic trial, are thrown into Stammheim prison in Stuttgart. They are eventually charged with four murders and 54 attempted murders. Stammheim is where it ends. On 9 May 1976 Ulrike Meinhof is found hanging in her cell. Thousands attend her funeral. On 18 October 1977 – in the midst of a heightened terror blitz that becomes known as the 'German Autumn' – Gudrun Ensslin and Andreas Baader are found dead in their cells.

By late 1996 a lot of the ground work has been done. The eponymous 'Baader Meinhof' single has been released – to some acclaim and some head scratching. Black Grape have put out an album – *It's Great When You're Straight . . . Yeah!* – with a pop art take on Carlos the Jackal's iconic photo on the front cover. Surely the world is ready for my deathly slow, handclapping, synth-squealching ogre-funk opus in praise of 70s terrorism. Surely?

The album starts, as all great albums do, with tape hiss – deliberate, anachronistic and ominous. Improbable as a human beatbox, I supply live handclaps and a vocal about Rudi Dutschke and the right-wing Springer press. I wrote most of this first version of the title track from memory – that is, no Red Army Faction study aids yet; just what I recall from those childhood news reports and any other titbits picked up on the way. The second song on the album, 'Meet Me at the Airport', is directly inspired by my altercation with the Scottish anarchist.

Track three, 'There's Gonna Be an Accident', is a kind of elegy to among others Petra Schelm, the first RAF member to lose her life (at 19 years of age when she is shot dead as her BMW smashes through a roadblock in Hamburg). 'Mogadishu' may be one of the most specific tracks on the album: a hallucinogenic fantasy about a Lufthansa plane hijacked in October 1977. Side one finishes with the short and necessarily throwaway track 'Burn Warehouse Burn', named after a Kommune 1, situationist-style communiqué.[39] 'GSG 29' opens side two – this is very much an album meant to exist on vinyl – with nothing you can't hear elsewhere: a collage of looped sounds from all the other tracks on the album. 'It's a Moral Issue' is an anomaly and has almost nothing to do with the RAF or any kind of terrorism. It's a self-reflexive ditty concerning a journalist, Steve Albini and Kurt Cobain. Nuff said. Natch, as they used to say in the *NME*. 'Kill Ramirez' is all about Carlos, known to his friends as fat boy. Of course, no terrorist-themed record would be complete without a song for the pin-up girl of guerrilla warfare, Leila Khaled, and I manage to sneak her into the last verse along with her dead co-hijacker, Patrick Arguello. I love the title track of the album so much that I decide to write it again, expanding on the impressionist lyric and this time recording it as a low-slung groover. *Baader Meinhof*. The myth. The legend. The album.[40]

Baader Meinhof, to all intents and purposes a solo album, is released to perplexed reviews in November 1996. *Q* magazine claims the album is 'jerrybuilt' – it is. The *Guardian* claims that I have wasted some of my best music on impenetrable subject matter – one third true. *Select* and *Melody Maker* both print sizeable rave reviews, the former even comparing me to George Clinton. Never a truer word. The *NME*, on predictable form, does its best to ignore the album for as long as possible, before commissioning a postage

[39] Kommune 1: the first political activist commune in West Berlin. Founded January 1967. Dubbed the 'horror commune' by the right-wing press.
[40] The original title for the album: *This Is the Hate Socialist Collective* is for some reason greeted with strong disapproval from Hut Recordings. So it becomes *Baader Meinhof*.

stamp 5/10 review in which their man wisely advises the readers to study Hanif Kureishi instead. *NME* sister mag *Vox* chimes in with another 5/10 and concludes that I may possibly be a 'twat'. These decidedly mixed notices all seem to think that a) I am being deliberately obscurantist, and b) there is a moral somewhere in these songs, which I have, again deliberately and quite wrongly, chosen to obfuscate. I am and there isn't.

John Cale's backing band are hiding in the dressing room – our dressing room – at La Cigalle theatre on a freezing late-November evening in Paris. I have played this venue many times, but this time am support to the great viola-bothering Welshman, apparently at his request. It's only the second live outing for my new Baader Meinhof Gruppe – actually me and a bunch of session players, but that's the way I like it now: two drummers – like the Glitter Band – two string players, tablas and Malcom Ross on bass. What a coup: I've got the Josef K guitar legend in my band and I've made him play the fucking bass. Oh well. It's a fine outfit nonetheless. Shame they will only play one more gig – supporting new terrors called Placebo in front of an audience of squealing ingrates. Cale's thrown a dark wobbler and broods alone in his lavish dressing room, one of his band having committed the unforgivable crime of allowing a small amount of electrical crackle to emit from a guitar lead during the soundcheck. Now the band are banished to our dressing room – where the party is. I sit in the corner with Momus and we yabber on about how great Cale occasionally is, and Euroterrorism this, Euroterrorism that. I am aware that we won't be able to do this again. We have a short French tour booked in as Baader Meinhof in the New Year, but even now I know that I have no real intention of seeing it through.

28

Fan club

December 1996. Spice Girls have the Christmas number one. The Auteurs' After Murder Park *is top ten in both* Select *and* Q *magazine writers' albums of the year poll. It is nowhere to be seen in the* NME *or* Melody Maker *albums of the year.*

There is a certain type of music fan who is compelled to own every last cough and dribble of released or unreleased product by their hero: the obsessive. No real harm in that at all; we've all been there, haven't we? Then there is the type of music fan whose obsession has run its natural course, so after maybe buying three or four albums, all the singles, all the limited editions and getting the autographs of the whole band, something happens: the artist releases a record that the fan does not like, or perhaps the artist is quoted saying something that the fan does not agree with. Now, instead of maybe taking the record back to the shops and getting a refund, or even just filing it away maybe to give it another spin in a few months' time, or putting the contentious quote down to the fact that the artist is just a silly pop star, the fan – we can now insert the word 'crazed' in front of 'fan' – goes ballistic. This shoddy album/terrible thing that has been said in the national press is obviously a slight against me, thinks crazed fan. It just exacerbates how awful the world really is and how everything and everyone is against me. Instead of going to see a doctor, crazed fan then proceeds to send a home-made nail bomb to the object of their obsession. Finally crazed fan has a choice of either filming his/her own suicide or going out and attempting to assassinate the president of the United States of America.

'I really need to talk to you.'

'Hi, did you enjoy the show?' I ask.

'No, you don't understand. I really, really need to talk to you . . .'

You're right, I don't understand. So what do I say to the fans? How about 'You've got great taste.' What else can I possibly say?

December '96. From the balcony of the Institute of Contemporary Arts the view of the Mall is fabulous. My late-November reverie is ruined by six words. 'I really need to talk to you,' the Anita Pallenberg lookalike says with great earnestness into my shell-like. Oh God, those words.

I try and humour the rock chick but she's not buying.

'I wanna join your band,' says Anita.

'Sure, you can join my band if you want. What do you play?' I say, thinking this gambit will catch her off guard.

'Not your band, I want to join your Baader Meinhof gang,' she demands. Not caught off guard at all.

'I'm not in the Baader Meinhof gang. They don't really exist any more; they pretty much ceased activities in the 80s,' I find myself reasoning with the lunatic.

'But I want to hurt people,' says the lunatic, as I stop reasoning and head back inside, where I have a clear run towards the stairs.

'I want to hurt people and I want to hurt you badly, and then I will throw myself from this balcony,' says the deranged Rolling-Stones-girlfriend doppelgänger.

I walk off, away from the volley of abuse that is now being hurled at me. There's no reasoning with a demented idiot. None at all. As I walk out the front doors of the ICA I look up into the calm winter night to the balcony several floors above. All is quiet. Sadly Miss Anita hasn't carried out her threat.

When the Auteurs return to the UK after the January 1995 tour of Japan, the freaky cultish behaviour of Suki X continues to play on my mind. Then, on 20 March of that year, the Aum Shinrikyo death cult comes down from Mount Fuji and launches a sarin attack on the Tokyo subway. Twelve commuters are killed, 54 seriously injured and 980 are affected. Before the attacks Aum had a membership exceeding 9000. Was Miss X involved in Aum Shinrikyo?

Almost two years later and a couple of ghosts from the past come back to haunt me. The packages that arrive in the post – delivered directly to my address – contain letters and gifts: broken vinyl – Auteurs albums – painted and cut into yin and yang shapes. The accompanying letters – there are three – start off with the predictable confessions of self-harm in Suki X's inimitable broken English and conclude with veiled threats, both physical and psychological, towards me. All this and a letter I receive from an old acquaintance accusing me of all sorts of miserable stuff draws me to conclude that after an interesting 12 months I may not be about to have the greatest end to my year.

Happy fucking Christmas. I had gathered that with two 'difficult' albums under my belt my popularity had taken a bit of a knock, but Jesus, this is getting quite ridiculous. Not only am I unpopular, now I am actively unpopular. I decide that the worst thing to do would be to go on tour in France. I don't want to add to my collection of suicidal Anitas and murderous Suki Xs. Alice has booked to go to Ireland for a few weeks, to contemplate our dying relationship, while I am due to be on tour with Baader Meinhof. The warning signs are all in place. I make a call to my old friends Robert and Brenda Allen. The time is right to get out of London for a while.

29

Quiet night in

January 1997. Townes Van Zandt dies of a heart attack on New Year's Day. David Bowie turns 50. Tori Amos, Whitetown and Blur all have number-one singles during January.

If normal service was now operational, I would be not be stifling my compulsion to convulse with laughter. But it isn't, and I am. There are just three of us sat around the kitchen table in Robert Allen's cold farmhouse near Leith Hill, Surrey. Robert, me and a gentleman in his late fifties (Robert's wife Brenda is out for the evening judging an under-12s martial arts competition at the church hall). I have been staying at the farmhouse with Robert and Brenda for the past few weeks and they have been providing solid entertainment for me, with a ever-changing and increasingly fucked-up conveyor belt of guests. At the front of the main farmhouse is a footpath that leads through several allotment patches. At the end of these smallholdings is a one-bedroom stone cottage originally intended for itinerant farm labourers – the lowest of the low. Joining us at the dinner table tonight is the cottage's current resident, Robert and Brenda's lodger. Astor Hollingshurst, though still in possession of a certain amount of faded elegance and wiry for his years, has clearly seen better days. Prior to Astor arriving, Robert takes me aside and conspiratorially tells me that Hollingshurst is lying low – 'A bit of bother with the fellows from Customs and Excise.' That makes two of us.

Astor Hollingshurst: a tall man with a tall story to tell. A psychedelic evangelist who claims to be a friend of Dr Timothy Leary. Robert and I catch each other stifling giggles several times during the, er, trip that the fruitcake is now, er, laying upon us. Arriving in mid-60s London with a jar of Owsley acid and a whole wad of cash that he had stolen from Leary, Astor brought one more thing into swinging London – a colossal heroin habit. As the money starts to run out and the dealing starts to increase, Hollingshurst's Cambridge Gardens flat – where else? – gets some unwanted attention. Astor is soon busted for dealing pot and amphetamine sulphate.

He receives a sentence of six years in the Scrubs, where he eventually meets Gerry Lime, who is, according to our dinner guest, 'Inside on a trumped-up possession charge. Prison was full of heads in the late 60s, you know,' adds Hollingshurst, to my and Robert's delight.

Now this Gerry Lime freak was a disciple of Dutch trepanation guru Dr Bart Hughes. Upon his release from prison, Lime decides that he wants a permanent high – also, he is fed up with 'getting busted' – so he drills a hole in his head.

'I suppose you could say I saw a business opportunity,' says Mr Hollingshurst as he picks up Robert's old acoustic guitar from the kitchen table.

'Robert tells me you're in the music industry.' He turns to me.

'Kind of,' I say.

'What do you think of this? Gerry and I wrote it in prison. It's part of a musical about trepanning,' says Astor Hollingshurst.

Oh God, I think as the oldest swinger in town starts to swing.

> Brain blood volume
> Open up the door
> Bore hole bore hole
> The order of the bore

The psychedelic reprobate repeats the chant-like dirge a few more times. I can't tell whether it's meant to be funny. I look over at Robert Allen, stoned and trying hard not to giggle, and feel my perspective lurch.

'What d'ya think?'

'I think you've put something in my drink,' I say to the counter-cultural chancer, as he puts down the guitar and picks up a battered attaché case.

'Old habits die hard,' says the dinner guest. 'I can tell you need to relax more.'

He opens up the case and with a flourish pulls out a saw-tooth drill.

'I studied theology inside. Would you like me to say a prayer? I'm also a lay preacher.'

Robert is laughing hysterically as I start tripping.

By early 1997 all the art has been done. This, I realise with the release of the *Baader Meinhof* album. Its reception, commercial and critical, is unimportant. The mission has been completed. Even though I am now rudderless – a man out of time – the record company want me to record new material. Perhaps as an antidote to the *BM* album – y'know, something that could actually sell.

The Verve are about to break into the mainstream. Surely if it can be achieved with them, then it could happen for the Auteurs. They just have to be A & R'ed properly, go back to writing about showgirls and Lenny Valentinos, maybe add a string section.

What they don't know is that I already consider the first two Auteurs albums commercial successes and I believe I have the ability to slip in and out of the mainstream at will. What I am now doing is making wilfully anti-commercial music and taking it to the very edge of the charts – like a vagrant walking up the garden path then lurking on the patio while inside the bourgeois dinner party continues as normal, trying to ignore the bitter face pressed against the French window sneering at them.

Anyway, the record company's demands will have to wait. Everything will have to wait. At the end of January I am scheduled to tour France, in my Baader Meinhof guise. The French agent, having witnessed the Cale show in Paris at the end of last year, got very excited and booked in a string of dates. There are only two small problems: a) the *Baader Meinhof* album is only 29 minutes long and there is no other material to draw on (29 minutes not really being enough to sustain an entire tour), and b) I need to get away from the crazies. Luckily Robert and Brenda have invited me to stay with them indefinitely. Robert is nine years older than me, the recipient of an inheritance and the heir to a curiosity that sometimes leads to bad things happening. I have no intention of going on tour. I have every intention of going to stay with my friend in his Surrey farmhouse to help him avoid the bad things that occasionally blight his life. (I also intend to avoid the bad things that are blighting my own life.)

On the eve of the tour I go AWOL in a move that I hope will provoke the record company into dropping me and also alienate me further from the musicians I work with. At just gone six on

Thursday evening I catch a commuter train from Waterloo station to Dorking. Half an hour later I get off at Dorking. After a ten-minute wait I am inside a minicab heading into the Surrey night towards the North Downs. It's only six or seven miles from the town but, to me at least, it feels like the wilderness. I pay the cab driver and walk the short distance up the lane to the farmhouse. Through the front window I can see a slight woman in her mid-thirties enthusiastically throwing punches and doing high kicks as part of her daily karate practice.

The three of us – Robert, me and the crazy acid priest – are now in the upstairs bathroom of the stone cottage next door to the Allens' farmhouse. Hollingshurst is taking control, ordering us around – Robert purposefully clearing out any unnecessary bathroom clutter and me trying to shine an anglepoise lamp onto a chair that was recovered from a decommissioned passenger jet. We are, according to our new guru, 'creating a safe and relaxed environment in which to carry out a procedure'. Robert has decided he would like to be trepanned, and Astor Hollingshurst has decided that he is the man who will trepan him.

Didn't I come to Surrey to avoid such people and situations? This window of lucidity opens and quickly shuts.

'We'll just need some sheets and cauterising equipment and then the operating theatre will be ready,' announces the doctor.

I just run this sentence through my mind one more time, to make sure that was what was just said. Yep, it was. *Hahahaha.*

Robert and I catch each other's eyes, but manage to suppress our whoops.

'Anaesthetic is not required. Normally I would recommend the patient takes some form of hallucinogenic – one or two microdots, perhaps some mushroom tea. When the patient is pleasantly tripping the short procedure can commence – the trepan.' Hollingshurst does another flourish with the drill and looks like Bela Lugosi.

Robert and I fail to suppress our snorts of laughter. The amateur surgeon is irritated.

'Trepanation is designed to release pressure and restore the brain blood volume level to that of childhood, the time in one's life when the ego is instilled. With you it may be earlier, Mr Haines. Your friend has agreed to have the procedure, though I feel it may also be beneficial to you. I could uncork your head like a cheap bottle of wine,' says Hollingshurst mock-threateningly.

'Thanks,' I say. I'm on the upswing. I haven't taken psychedelics – of my own free will or otherwise – for years. I figure that this situation is so absurd I may as well enjoy it. At least I think that's what I think.

'Can I have some more acid, please?' I ask our new friend brightly.

'Good wisdom,' says Astor. 'Go to the kitchen and fetch me my coat.'

I look at Robert, now sat in the old aeroplane seat – the 'operating' chair – and think to myself how I must thank my friend for introducing me to such a lovely person. I stumble out the bathroom door and stand outside for a few seconds just to listen to the great preacher.

'I will make an incision here, the bore hole. With the drill I will remove a semicircle of bone, being careful not to penetrate the membrane. Penetration of the dura membrane will certainly cause permanent brain damage.'

'Oh,' says Robert.

Astor Hollingshurst. What a guy. Hurry along, don't want to miss this, I think to myself as I head next door, back to the main farmhouse, where Brenda has returned from her martial arts tournament and is making hot dogs for a couple of the karate kids. I do my best 'I am normal' walk to the kitchen table, not wanting to upset the children.

'You all right, darling, had a little too much wine?'

I don't answer, unsure of what might come out. I attempt a comforting smile.

'Oh dear,' says Brenda. 'Listen,' she continues, 'have you seen Robert? I need to talk to him about our tenant. The old guy keeps avoiding me. He owes us two months' rent. Have you seen him?'

'Yeah, he's next door. He's drilling a hole in Robert's head.' I was worried I might say something like that. Brenda's not sure what I'm talking about, but she has an inkling that something is about to go very wrong. The younger karate kid, a boy of about eight, looks like he's about to burst into tears.

'Kids, go and play in the front room; everything is going to be all right. Auntie Brenda is just going next door, to have a chat with Uncle Robert,' says Auntie Brenda. Then to me: 'Go to the pub. Get help.'

Is she telling me to just go to the pub, or is she saying have a drink, then get some psychiatric care for yourself? Or does she mean go to the pub, there are people there, bring them back here to help if things get nasty? Either way, it seems I have to go to the pub. Feeling galvanised and clear-headed, I rummage in Astor Hollingshurst's walletless inner coat pocket and find a strip of four microdots. I carefully tear one off and place it on my tongue, before wandering out into the night. To get help.

I have been standing outside the public bar of the Pig and Poke for a while now. I am having some trouble remembering what I am doing here. I know that Brenda sent me on some errand, but every time I scour my brain it just seems to throw up another existential dilemma. Like, am I the sort of person who's allowed in a public bar?

'Can I help you?' says the barman, opening the door but blocking my entrance.

Hold it together, I think, *hold it together*.

'I need a drink, and I need help,' I announce to the barman.

'We all do.' The barman smiles. 'Come in . . . and behave yourself,' he adds, obviously thinking that I do not look like too much of a wrong 'un, nothing he can't handle. *That went extremely well*, I think to myself, relieved that I have finally remembered why I am here.

I sit in the snug and decide that the best thing to do is keep an eye on the pint of stout and the glass of port that sit in front of me. A wise move, as the enfant terrible of Britart is walking over to my nice quiet table.

'Have you met my brother?' asks artist Jake Chapman as he sits down next to me. 'We call him the Dinos Twin, though he's not actually my twin.'

'Aloha,' says the Dinos Twin as he sits down, flanking me on the other side. Normally, I would not commend these brothers in art on their dress sense – country boys donning the casual togs of the leisured classes – but tonight they are looking sharp.

'Have you met our friend Robbie Williams?' says the Dinos Twin forcefully to me, as he pulls the brim of his Cavalier's hat over his eyes and adjusts an ostrich feather in the band. 'He's a huge star in the Royal Ballet.'

Robbie does an arabesque and pulls up a chair in front of me. *Wow. I've never seen someone move with such grace*.

I've never met a professional dancer before and there is so much I want to ask Robbie. But before I get the chance I am interrupted by Jake Chapman, who leans towards Robbie and whispers, 'Crispian is going to be here soon, mob-handed. The witch-finder general's been seen in the village. Tonight's the night.' Chapman then makes a cryptic sign with his right hand, revealing a long-handled dagger in his utility doublet. Robbie Williams takes the floor in the middle of this public house, and dances a wonderful interpretation of the letter K.

'Can he not speak?' I ask the Dinos Twin.

'He can not,' answers the artist. 'Crispian thought it better that we cut out his tongue.' I ponder this last statement. The Dinos Twin's suspicion has been aroused by my silence.

'Speak!' Shouts the older artist brother. 'Or never speak again.'

'Calm down, Dinos Twin,' says Jake, and turns to me. 'Now, fellah, tell us your name, and what Puritan business brings you here.'

I'm about to answer when I notice that the barman is shaking his head at me, trying to tell me something. I recognise this man: he is Lawrence from Denim.

As the clock chimes nine times, Crispian Mills, followed by the rest of Kula Shaker, bursts through the door of the Pig and Poke and rowdily orders ales.

Now I know the kind of people who drink in the public bar, I smirk to myself as Jake Chapman babbles excitedly in my ear.

'He's the man who made it all possible,' confides Chapman, nodding towards Mills. 'He's a brilliant man, a great man, not like me. Or the Dinos Twin,' he adds as an afterthought. 'Kula Shaker's platinum album *K* paved the way for our own *Great Deeds Against the Dead*,' continues Jake. 'There are some big changes in this land and in this county. Cromwell's days are numbered. The Shaker are a righteous cabal, intent on the preservation of the monarchy. The only man who shall dislodge the king of England from his throne is his son and rightful heir, who in good time will wear the royal crown.'

'Those are dangerous words, friend,' I say to the idiotic artist. 'Do you want a drink?' He doesn't, so I head to the bar to talk to Lawrence from Denim.

'A pint of stout and a port chaser please,' I say to the Brummie barman.

'Do not serve that man,' booms a voice from the other side of the bar.

I turn slowly. I know that voice, a voice that speaks with deep knowledge of the mysteries of the east. 'What d'ya want, Millsie?' I say.

'I want to know your name,' counters Crispian Mills.

'You and whose army?' I shoot back as Kula Shaker move towards me as one.

'We must know your name and what business brings you to these parts,' says someone from Kula Shaker more reasonably.

I take a deep breath as the alehouse falls into silence.

'My name is Matthew Hopkin. You may know me as the witch-finder general. My business is lancing the heathen boil of ungodliness that has spread through these parts of south England like a plague. I prick with my knife to find the mark of the witch. For the past two years I have travelled through the counties of East Anglia. I have put to death many a heathen. Now I find myself in Surrey and, so help me, there is much of the Lord's work to be done here. Is any man or woman in this alehouse foolish enough to stand in the way of God's will?' I scan the faces of the drinkers for those who would dare challenge my authority.

Justine Frischmann sits at the bar with some young mods, pre-occupied with a design magazine. The normally verbose Louise

Weiner from Sleeper keeps shtum. My confidence growing, I continue to goad.

'Well come on then. Is there one man, woman or child in this fucking alehouse who thinks that they're hard enough?'

A figure comes out of the gloom towards the fire. 'Aye, I'll take you on,' sneers Martin Rossiter, lead singer of Gene, breaking the silence. 'String him up!' he roars.

'Aye, string him up!' shout the Chapman Brothers in unison, as Robbie Williams' legs whirl towards me in a frenzied cartwheel attack.

'This way,' whispers a Brummie voice in my ear. Lawrence from Denim has sprung into action, smashing gas lamps and plunging the tavern into darkness. 'Jump,' monotones Lawrence. I obey, and vault the bar just as the singer produces a club from under the bar. 'Do you want sum of this, Millsie, ya posh southern twat,' says my saviour from the West Midlands, defending me, and his bar, from the lead singer of Kula Shaker and his band of marauding Cavaliers.

Lawrence has really come good this time, I think to myself as I grab a musket that hangs behind the bar. I climb through a trapdoor into the cellar, where I make my escape from the vigilante mob. I think about all the things I want to tell Lawrence: that I really like all the Denim albums and that this hasn't always been easy, as his previous outfit, Felt, always leant towards an awkward feyness that irritated (and it really didn't help when the singer from Belle and Sebastian said he was a big fan). Go Kart Mozart, Lawrence's future endeavour, will certainly have their moments. *But, Lawrence, none of this is worth losing your mind over. And I'm sorry I keep on laughing at you but, you know, you're Lawrence.*

On top of Leith Hill I survey the lie of the land. Beneath me the English countryside. The North Surrey Downs; to the west,

Guildford; to the north, London. The king's troops will be congregating at the alehouse, and the angry peasant mob will have set the dogs on my scent. If I run towards Reigate I can steal a horse. The dogs are getting closer. Water. If I cross water I will leave the dogs behind. But there is no water. I will run faster if I am naked, so I undress and throw my fashionable Puritan threads over the branches of a bare tree – a present for the dogs, to send them off my trail. In the distance beneath me I can see a beacon of hope, a farmhouse with light in its windows. Perhaps I can hide out in the barn. I sling the musket across my back and start running for my life.

I wake with a start and reach for my musket, but I have been disarmed by Brenda. 'You were in a bit of a state last night,' she says. 'We were about to send a search party out and then you turned up outside the house at 10.30 –'

'At least I wasn't too late getting in,' I interrupt, not entirely sure that I want to hear any more.

'– standing there naked, waving a branch from a tree, going on about Kula Shaker and a musket.'

'Where's Robert?' I interrupt again, parts of the evening coming back to me.

'He's sleeping it off,' says Robert's wife. 'Bad acid. He should be all right.'

'The same?' I ask.

'Yep. That Hollingshurst guy was down on his luck. He ended up with a very bad batch of acid he couldn't sell to anybody.'

'So what about the trepanation business?'

'Well,' says B, 'after I sent you off to "get help" – thanks so much for that by the way' – I grunt unenthusiastically at her sarcasm – 'I went round to the cottage and found Robert begging the old guy to drill a hole in his head. Hollingshurst just kept repeating that he wasn't in the habit of handing out freebies and it would cost a minimum of a grand. I told the shyster that I have a black belt in karate and I'd let him off the back rent if he pissed off now. So off he went with his tail between his legs this morning. And if anyone else wants a hole drilling in their head, I'll do it for free.'

It's time to stop pissing about. I decide to leave Leith Hill and go back to London. The music industry must by now be missing me. I spend the morning gathering up my possessions and trawling the surrounding countryside for any far-flung clothes. In the afternoon I bid the Allens a fond farewell. I tell them it's been swell and all, but I do not wish to see them for a long time. They fully concur. We must not do this again any time soon.

The cab wends its way through the country lanes, until we finally get to the sleepy civilisation of Dorking. At the traffic lights the cab driver points out some prisoners working in a chalk quarry below. I look down and see a tall gangly man having trouble controlling a wheelbarrow full of rocks, his bespectacled face looking up at me. The sad-eyed broken face of Jarvis Cocker, no longer the spear-wielding warrior, is staring into my eyes. And is that the hunched frame of Liam Gallagher moving one mound of dirt away from another mound of dirt. Two brothers with shaven heads snigger as they dig mini-trenches in the chalk and sand just big enough for a scaled-down re-enactment of the Battle of the Somme with model soldiers. Is this what happened at the end of the Britpop Nuremburg trials? Twenty years of hard labour in Dorking. I look one more time at the men working in the quarry. Within minutes the cab is outside the station. *At least I'm not breaking rocks*, I think as I get on board a train to London.

30

The rest of the world is laughing at us

February–March 1997. On 1 February Brian Connelly of the Sweet dies of kidney failure after years of alcohol abuse. U2 and No Doubt have number-one singles during the month. Mansun have a number-one album in March with Attack of the Grey Lantern *and Paul McCartney gets a knighthood.*

All bad things must come to an end and you don't have to be a visionary – though it does help – to see that by 1997 the wheels are about to come off the Britpop go-kart. Art has been replaced by something they call popular culture. It encompasses all things crass and vulgar: drugs, books written by Scotsmen, TV, cinema, comedy, public executions, plague, pestilence, death. Everything really. As a nation we are lost. Our forefathers would be most displeased.

What we need is a damn good war. Not just a grubby oil-robbing job out in the Middle East but a proper old dust-up between most of Europe and the baddies, so that by teatime Finland and Norway are at each other's throats. Most good art is born out of war. Dada as anti-art and anti-rationality, a direct response to the horrors of the First World War trenches, where no sane man would ever go. In the 20s the Dadaists became surrealists. Many of these artists had fought in the war and by the 30s saw that the whole gasket was about to blow again. Guernica, Wyndham Lewis (again), Christopher Isherwood. Perhaps the entire counterculture was a result of the Second World War, as the baby boomers entered the mystic in an attempt to avoid inheriting the sins of their parents. The problem by the mid-90s is that the old soldiers are dying out and the children of the baby boomers can only remember back as far as the mod revival of '79. And so in 1997 the children of punk clink glasses with the prime minister at a Downing Street champagne reception. When the grandeur of the moment has faded and the ignorant vulgarians are feeling, well, just a little foolish, they will protest *I only wanted to have a look round the gaff*. And look round they did. Happily for us every loving, obsequious gaze is caught on camera. Forever. So, children, wear your poppy with pride and while you're at it remember to write a good song.

Conditioned by years of featherweight religion, the public and media – always happy to believe in something that does not exist – have yet to twig that the so-called Britpop party is over. Unlike some of the main players. Elastica are in a sloth somewhere in self-induced narcoleptic oblivion. Pulp are working on an album called *We Don't Like Being Famous Anymore*. Blur have released a song called 'Beetlebum' which sounds like one of mine from a few years ago. Oasis, not content with disgracing themselves at the aforementioned vainglorious shenanigans in Downing Street, have released a dead-dog's dinner of an album, *Be Here Now*,[41] which by

[41] I should point out that, as of the time of writing – early twenty-first century – the author has not listened to the album in question and has no inclination to listen to said album. Therefore I will have to conclude that for once the consensus must be right. *Be Here Now* is indeed a dead-dog's dinner.

the twenty-first century (but not 1997) will become a byword for dead-dog's dinners. The lead singer from Kula Shaker will invoke the 'I'm a deluded rock star; I have been dabbling in mystic mumbo-jumbo and, with thudding predictability, am now going to reclaim the swastika as a sign of peace' clause, thus precipitating the cruel but necessary end to his career (his loss, our gain). American magazine *Vanity Fair* – with a front-cover photo of the singer from Oasis lying down with a blonde lady – will bestow the epithet 'Cool Britannia' upon this once-noble nation. People who normally sneer and carp at everything the yanks say or do take this very seriously.

Of course *I* saw it all coming. *What d'ya mean Oasis have blown it? Could have told you that before the first album came out, etc*. I'm an old boxer swinging on the ropes, just trying to conserve a bit of energy.

So, how am I taking advantage of these chinks in the armour? By tearing down the walls of Jericho of course. On returning from my trip to the countryside, I decide that the best way to meet the world of showbiz head on is to write and record a concept album about telekinetic children – *ESP Kids*. By March '97, after tens of thousands of record-company pounds have been spent in the studio, the album will be entirely aborted – to the relief of Virgin Records, who certainly don't want another concept album to flog. I am also playing guitar and glockenspiel in a folk group. Maybe I'm playing the long game, but the Walls of Jericho remain upstanding.

Balloon are a fine group. A fine group with one absolute 24-carat, I'd-kill-to-have-written-that song in their armoury, 'Underneath My Bed', a two-and-a-half-minute list of hoarded ephemera: the eyes of Robert Capa, the legs of Eric Morecambe, the hat of Tommy Cooper. Phil Vinall, by now becoming something of a patron saint of lost causes, hooked me up with this bunch at the end of '96.

I have one aim – to help them record 'Underneath My Bed' and turn it into the classic it so obviously can be. There is, as ever, a snag. Balloon have been around the track once before, having recorded an expensive album in the early 90s that didn't do any real business. The band then disappeared for a few years, forgotten but not forgiven. To have had big-label backing in the music industry and then to have failed is bad form, like streaking at Lord's and no one noticing.[42] Balloon have a couple of other problems: an unavoidable folkie bent (in five years' time this would be de rigueur, but right now no chance) and the fact that none of the other material, good as it is, sounds anything like 'Underneath My Bed'. Balloon are a one-song band. One great song, and that's no mean feat. Few can honestly claim to have one great song. Noel Gallagher cannot, for sure. So Balloon rehearse and play gigs, and I forget that I am meant to have a career elsewhere. I just want a record company to notice 'Underneath My Bed'. They don't. By now, however, I have noticed the charismatic female backing singer – who shouldn't be a backing singer at all – and the funny old gentleman with a pencil moustache who turns up at Balloon rehearsals to play the musical saw.

[42] Failure is only really acknowledged when an artist has been dropped by a prominent record label.

31

New girl in town revisited

May–November 1997. *Take That have gone but Barlow manages a number-one single in May. In June Ronnie Lane dies and* The *Verve have a number one with 'The Drugs Don't Work'. Radiohead release* OK Computer, *and throughout August and September Oasis are number one in the album charts. On 6 November ex-Swell Map Epic Soundtracks dies. David Bowie, Bono, et al. have a number-one single with Lou Reed's ode to joy, 'Perfect Day'.*

After helping Balloon out by not succeeding in securing them a recording contract, I do the decent thing and have a rummage through the dying embers of the band. The correct term to describe this not entirely selfless act is asset stripping, through you could call it grave robbing. Predictably, and perhaps rightly, this act generates a certain amount of ill feeling among various parties. The Lord giveth and the Lord taketh away.

A Balloon rehearsal is like a music industry halfway house. One half of the room is like a reception lounge, where keen young people, unspoilt by the realities of the industry, are eager to tread the boards in the back rooms of London pubs, hoping that one day, by a stroke of fortune, a stray *NME* reviewer may pass solemn judgement, perhaps noticing the grace in those nimble fingers as they dart across a piano keyboard, or how the sassy swish of a bass line adds hitherto unheard-of gravitas and is actually the making of the goddamn song. Young dreams. The other half of the rehearsal studio is a waiting room, where old campaigners huddle close together, grimly aware that now they have been cast out of the gates of the city, any new dawn is most likely to be a false one. It won't be long before some of these old soldiers can no longer put off the inevitable – writing for a music monthly. So, it is in the reception room that I meet Sarah Nixey and the waiting room where I meet John Moore.

Moore, like me, is a veteran. In the late 80s John Moore's star was, for a nanosecond, in the ascendant as only the third in the long and noble line of Jesus and Mary Chain drummers. At the vital moment when the Mary Chain looked like they were going to go cornflakes, young Moore jumped the (soon to be sinking very, very slowly) ship.[43] Naughty. Having blagged a huge record deal with chutzpah and big hair, the cheeky drummer recorded some colossally un-cheap albums in some of America's finest recording studios as an odd sort of Billy Idol/Alan Vega carve-up and went to live out his rock 'n' roll dreams in the Chelsea Hotel. The public, however, were not ready for such far-sighted un-selfconscious shenanigans, giving the recorded oeuvre of John Moore and the Expressway the big thumbs down.

By the mid-90s Moore had returned to London. Out of a deal and living in penury, he decided to tell the Britpop loving

[43] No slight on the Mary Chain. Enoch Powell said that all political careers end in failure. The same is mostly true of rock bands.

masses all about his woes via an album of quiet, clever meditations about suicide called, rather wonderfully, *You Might As Well Live*. Moore meant to call his group Siberia but ended up with Revolution 9. By 1996 JM had put his suicidal tendencies on hold to do what all underachievers inevitably do: a) learn an exotic instrument, the saw, and b) reintroduce absinthe – the potent wormwood spirit that helped turn the French army myopic during the First World War – to Britain via the Czech Republic in a (hopefully deliberate) attempt to destroy London's chattering classes.

It starts out, as all things do, with a damn good band name: Black Box Recorder. Moore comes up with the name after a bumpy flight back from Spain – he will later tell the press that the plane actually crashed. So, with little more than a fine band name, Moore and I move the concept out of the alehouse and onto the next level: the clanging of tin cans. Oh yes, Black Box Recorder shall be an art house sonic terror assault duo. *Haven't I been here before?* Luckily, the small record label which has agreed to bankroll this 'project' pulls out after a last-minute hiccup from its backers, or possibly they just came to their senses. So once again the world is deprived of the chance to listen to me blowing into a goat horn over a backing track of white noise approximating the sound of an aircraft crashing – at this rate I'm never going to get reviewed in *The Wire*. And that should have been the end of the matter, but Moore is persistent. With my, er, profile relatively higher than his, this ex-tub-thumper from the 80s isn't going to let me go in a hurry and we soon have another recording session booked – this one gratis, care of Shakin' Stevens' ex-drummer. As unpromising as this may seem, things are actually on the upturn.

Approach with extreme caution. The danger has not passed.

With Shaky's drummer on standby and Moore and myself on collision course with some expensive recording equipment, we are still extremely likely to commit a crime of the musically experimental nature. Black Box Recorder needs a song. 'Girl Singing in the Wreckage' pops out of nowhere, an old-fashioned death song about a teenage girl and her baby, possibly the only survivors of an air crash. A slight number that doesn't bother trying too hard. I hand over a half-finished lyric sheet to Moore for his contribution and within 20 minutes we've got a complete song. Fortunately we've accidentally written a song that only a female can sing.

I've had the pin between my fingers for a while now, but the time has come to burst the balloon. But John Moore is already scrawling a fax to Sarah Nixey. *Best not dwell too much on Moore's past*, I think, as he writes with no trace of irony, 'We've written you a fabulous song. Please come and sing it and we will make you famous.'

Sarah Nixey is our Trojan horse. The rose between the thorns, with the voice of Sweet Mother Mary. At 23 years old she's still young enough to believe at least half the bullshit that Moore and I indiscriminately fling about. She's also young enough and willing enough to learn a little bit about cruelty, the lifeblood of Black Box Recorder. Nixey is one of the reasons that the phone has started ringing again. When Nixey walks into a room, men fall hopelessly and uselessly in love. A useful asset for a band.

Shaky's drummer (Chris Wyles) and Phil Vinall have done a good job recording 'Girl Singing in the Wreckage', so good in fact that a tape of the track has been anonymously sent out to various record companies, whom it would seem are rather hot to trot. Hut wants us to record more tracks for an EP. This would be the easiest course of action, but now other labels are showing an interest – not knowing of my involvement of course. It is becoming clear that a healthy advance for everyone is imminent. But not from Hut. Given my previous track record, David Boyd has his hands tied and knows that he cannot squeeze any more money from the shareholders until I deliver a commercial Auteurs album. I decide not to wait for this momentous occasion. So I am free to go and sign with another label and, here's the good bit, I get to retain my contract with Virgin. For me life is just getting better and better. The rest of the country is about to enthusiastically saddle itself with a new prime minister, one who likes walking around with dumb trophy pop stars on his arm. Oh well, the peasants seem happy enough – for the moment.

It comes to me, if not in a dream then in a moment of clarity, on a late-spring morning. A nagging chant rattles through my head as I slowly wake up. *Life is unfair, life is unfair, life is unfair*. On and on it goes, needling and chiding, until I can take no more. There's only one riposte to counter this oh so sorry for itself sentiment: *Kill yourself or get over it*. Where on earth have I heard this before? Jones? Koresh? Maybe Robert de Grimston and the Process Church of the Final Judgement? As I begin to shake off my bleariness, I notice the meaning of the words and realise with some sadness that if no pseudo-religion has a credo quite like this, then yes, it must have come out of my own imagination. So 'Child Psychology' – with verses written by John Moore – gets a chorus and I get to make another record that won't be played on the radio.

Luke Haines is alive and kicking and Britpop is dead. Baader Meinhof was a one-off. The Auteurs are cryogenically frozen, and Black Box Recorder are now the real deal. According to some, Black Box Recorder commenced the recording of their debut LP, *England Made Me*, on May Day 1997. Not so, that would give May

Day '97 far more gravitas than it deserves. The recordings are done in short bursts throughout the year, paid for by smash-and-grab raids on our many prospective suitors within the music industry. Demo money: Island, Warners, EMI and Universal all cough up and help to finance a record that none of them will actually release. Finally in late '97 a man called Gordon Biggins is made head of A & R at revamped Chrysalis Music. Gordon Biggins has two wishes. The first is to make Chrysalis a cool label again, like when they had, y'know, er, Blondie. The second is for people to stop making stupid anagrams of his name. Big Gordon's Gin, anyone? Biggins, like David Boyd, is a rare fellow of some integrity. We present Chrysalis with a finished album that they have not contributed one bean towards. They give us a lucrative advance. Biggins even thinks, much to our astonishment, that 'Child Psychology' will make a fine first single. In December '97 Black Box Recorder signs with Chrysalis. I now have two recording contracts, both with major labels. In mid-'96 I was dropped by my publishers and at the beginning of this year (1997) things were extremely rocky with Virgin. I'm like the new girl in town, and once again everyone wants to fuck me.

The commercial success that this plethora of recording contracts garners is negligible. Black Box Recorder will go on to make some unimprovable records that are sometimes even liked by broader sections of the general public. The concept of success itself is of course debatable. Was Kurt Cobain's existence a terrible failure in comparison to the miserable yet fully realised life of Muhammad Atta? the most pleasing aspect of the end of 1997 is how readily the stars of Britpop are falling by the wayside, though some, unfortunately, seem to be in it for the long haul.

Over the next few years I keep up the one-label-for-me, one-label-for-BBR juggling trick and cease to acknowledge the glories and travails of my contemporaries. *Art can only thrive in hermetically sealed conditions*. Remember? Occasionally I get to stand on the precipice of success, have a look down then head back. I am a cell of one. It's the best way to be.

Postscript

As a nation we have truly lost our way

August 1997. The hammer is quite beautiful, the steel head sharp and shiny, the handle bound in leather. The hammer is part one of a present from Steve Albini. The second part of the gift is a CD of Elton John's poignant reworking of 'Candle in the Wind'. A tribute to the now one-week-dead-but-still-not-in-the-ground Princess of Wales – England's rose, apparently. The previous Sunday had seen the prime minister put the final nail in the Cool Britannia coffin, jettisoning the pesky pop stars and delivering a lip-trembling nation-united-in-grief speech with the ultimate trophy girlfriend on his arm – a dead princess. I know what I'm supposed to do with the hammer and CD combination, but I just can't. I have a soft spot for Elton's industriousness – boy, he recycled that tune sharpish.

It's been a fine summer. The Black Box Recorder album is almost finished, and I am now working on what will become a new Auteurs album – what was to be The Commercial One. Of course everything has now been turned on its head. Hut has heard the BBR album and thinks it's going to sell – this an album that they were not prepared to dig deep in their pockets for, so consequently do not own. David Boyd is perhaps worried that after all these years of careless nurture I may take all my toys elsewhere, so he's not going to be too pushy. The result of all these mind games and petty paranoias is that the pressure is off. I can do what the hell I like. The goalposts have been moved, and I am the only one pretending to know where they've been moved to. Naturally, with my almost biblical desire for revenge, I am fairly pleased with the situation.

Everything you see on the TV is true. Everything you read about in newspapers is also true. Saturday, 6 September: funeral day. I have decided to go out and catch a little bit of this national mourning that the TV and radio have been banging on about all week. Since being knocked out of the 1996 European Natious Cup to the tune of 'Three Lions' Britain has got awfully keen on stewing in its national mood. So I elect to take a walk around my Camden manor to see how the other half lives.

The Adidas-wearing mods have been eaten alive by the dough-faced peasants from the Midlands, who push prams stuffed with pudgy offspring along Camden High Street and are eager to do a few tourist spots before lining the path of the funeral cortège. The drug dealers are lying low, hiding out from the flesh-hungry mutant families from Essex led by roaring fat bald men wielding sticks and dressed in shorts. Make no mistake there is a national mood: anger. The people have congregated in the capital to mourn the passing of their dead new figurehead, and the nation has seen with its own eyes . . . that it has been beaten around the head very badly with the ugly stick. Very badly indeed. The nation is not happy about it. Not one bit.

I continue my trek up Camden's Parkway to Regent's Park then on to Primrose Hill. This elite enclave of north-west London – where only the singer from Texas can afford to live – has been overrun by provincial zombies from Northshire. I decide that my best route of escape will be over the railway bridge towards Chalk Farm; surely the cretin crusade could not have advanced this far. I walk down the hill until I come to a set of traffic lights at the junction by the old Roundhouse. I stand on the pavement waiting to cross the road and a white van pulls up beside me. I stare across the road, trying to gauge how many grief-struck proles I will have to wade through, when I spy a familiar face eating a lolly outside Marine Ices: Noel Gallagher. Oh Christ. The contents of the white van have seen him too.

'Oi, Noel!' shouts the driver as the lights change to green. 'Fookin' mad for it!' he yells as the van speeds off round the corner.

Noel looks across the road and sees only me. He smiles and gives me a friendly wave. In just over a month's time I will be 30 years old. I raise my left hand and wave back weakly as Noel takes a bite from his lolly.

Acknowledgements

. . . THEN: Alice Readman, Phil Vinall, Glenn Collins, Barney C. Rockford, James Banbury, all Auteurs/Baader Meinhof auxiliary. David Boyd, Ken Marshall and all at Hut Recordings. Phill Savidge, John Best, Best in Press, Savidge and Best and all those who served there. Steve Albini, Pete Hofmann, Tony Beard, Jon Eydmann, Brett Anderson, Bernard Butler, Matt Osman, Simon Gilbert. Finally, in true Mott tradition, my chance to thank the road crew: Mikey, Mr Mick Brown, Adam and Big Neil.

. . . AND NOW: Thank you to Clare Conville and all at Conville and Walsh for their enthusiasm and wisdom. Jason Arthur, my editor, and all at William Heinemann. Garry Boorman at CEC Management. John Moore, Sarah Nixey and all BBR auxiliary. Charlie Inskip and Stefan De Batselier. All my love of course to Mrs Solanas – who has had to read this book many, many times – and to Fred who, thankfully, cannot yet read.